# *Your Next Move*

# Your
# ●●● Next
# Move

**Everything
You Want
to Know
About Jobs,
State Benefits,
Self-Employment**

*Philip Pedley and Paul McEvoy*

KOGAN
PAGE

First published in 1994

Kogan Page Limited
120 Pentonville Road
London N1 9JN

© Philip Pedley and Paul McEvoy 1994

**British Library Cataloguing in Publication Data**

A CIP record for this book is available from the British Library.

ISBN 0–7494–1265–8

Typeset by DP Photosetting, Aylesbury, Bucks
Printed and bound in Great Britain by
Clays Ltd, St Ives plc

# Contents

Introduction   9

1. **Definitions of Unemployment and Redundancy**
   **(Where do you fit in?)**   11
   Voluntary redundancy *11*
   Compulsory redundancy *12*
   Early retirement *13*
   Termination and dismissal *14*
   Negotiating the best deal when leaving *18*

2. **A Guide to State Benefits (Some help through**
   **the maze)**   21
   Unemployment Benefit *21*
   Income Support *24*
   Sickness and Invalidity Benefits *25*
   Statutory redundancy *26*
   State help for getting back to work *28*
   Other State benefits in brief *30*
   Recap *30*
   Proposed future changes *31*

3. **Your Financial Situation – Taking Action**   33
   Signing on *33*
   Household and personal finances *33*
   Taking legal advice *35*
   Holding on to your lump sum *36*

4. **Assessing Your Job Prospects**   37
   Analysis of your employment capabilities *37*
   Trends in recruitment *39*
   Choosing the right job *42*

5. **Training Opportunities**   44
   The types of qualification available *44*
   Finding training opportunities and method of
      learning *47*

Financing your training and education *48*
Training and Enterprise Councils and Local Enterprise
  Companies *51*

6. **Setting Your Sights for Employment**                    **55**
The CV *55*
Where to find jobs *62*
Organising your day *68*
The age barrier: some alternatives to getting
  a job *69*

7. **Preparing for an Interview**                            **72**
The purpose of an interview *72*
Preparation *73*
The day of the interview *74*

8. **The Interview**                                         **78**
Open and closed questions *79*
Pressure questions *79*
Moral-dilemma questions *80*
Tests *81*

9. **Interview Questions: A Practical Example**              **84**
The opening *84*
Chronological review *84*
The personality probe *85*
Recap *86*
If you fail! *87*

10. **Starting Your Own Business**                           **88**
Is it a feasible option? *88*
Categories of business *88*
Initial research *89*
Predicting financial viability *90*
Identifying possible business ventures *91*
Ways of running your own business *100*
Help in setting up your business *102*

11. **Working or Retiring Abroad**                           **105**
Employment in the European Community *105*
Retiring in the European Community *108*
Working outside the European Community *109*
Retirement outside the European Community *110*

**12. Investing for the Future**     **113**
    Tax issues *113*
    Investing your money *114*

*Index*     *119*

# Introduction

This book is aimed at helping you if you have been, or are being, faced with redundancy, unemployment or early retirement. It aims to give you the background to the choices and options available to you. Depending on your circumstances the range of statutory rights, State benefits and choices will obviously vary. We will cover subjects such as organising yourself, the problem of morale and how to get a job. We also realise that because of age or circumstances you may not want a job. If this is the case, what are the options open to you? Have you considered living abroad? What about starting your own business? Is retraining an option?

Please note that United Kingdom telephone numbers are due to change on 16 April 1995. After that date, please check any numbers in this book that you plan to use.

# 1
# Definitions of Unemployment and Redundancy (Where do you fit in?)

It's important you take the time to sit down and decide what your circumstances actually are. Once you have done this you will be in a position to determine the sort of action which best suits you. This chapter attempts to provide a breakdown of the different categories of redundancy or unemployment which you might face. These questions are vitally important in determining the State benefits you may be entitled to.

If you suspect you are about to be made unemployed this chapter will give you guidance on how to proceed and the preparations you need to make. Again, the way you choose to respond to your employer can have all sorts of financial and legal consequences.

If you have just been made unemployed use this chapter to check whether your former employer has acted in a proper manner. Just because you have resigned or 'accepted' the terms offered by your ex-employer does not mean you do not have the right to challenge those terms.

What follows is an attempt to define the different categories which may be listed as:

1. Voluntary redundancy
2. Compulsory redundancy
3. Early retirement
4. Termination and dismissal.

We have added a further section which we believe you should read at this stage.

5. Negotiating the best deal when leaving.

## Voluntary redundancy

Redundancy is dismissal caused by the need to reduce a workforce. Voluntary redundancy occurs when an employer decides it is over-staffed for whatever reason and rather than embarking on a programme of compulsory redundancy (see below) the employer asks for volunteers who are prepared to give up their jobs in return for a benefits package. This will normally involve a lump-sum payment. Usually, but not always, voluntary redundancy is directed at older employees and the redundancy package will be tied in with an early retirement pension (see below).

The offer of a voluntary redundancy package is not necessarily an unattractive option for a younger employee. For example, an employee may be sufficiently confident that his or her skills will enable him or her to find a new job very quickly. If this is the case a lump-sum payment will obviously be most welcome. However, unless you are supremely confident of obtaining another job, this course is a gamble. One exception is if you feel your particular skills lend themselves to your establishing your own business, in which case the lump-sum payment can provide the means for financing the new venture. If you think the self-employed route is for you then do your sums carefully. Prepare a business plan and establish whether the lump-sum payment will be enough to finance your proposed business and your living costs. For more ideas on this, see Chapter 10.

## Compulsory redundancy

As the term suggests this is redundancy without an option. In this situation your employer may communicate to you the fact that your services are no longer required and should indicate the financial package that is being made available to you. Again, early retirement may well be part of the package. Compulsory redundancy may come 'out of the blue' or may follow rumours or an announcement that the company will be embarking on such a course. You may also be deemed to be redundant if your employer has laid you off and has stopped paying your wages. Either way you should take immediate steps to assess your circumstances and the appropriate action needed.

### Employers who go 'bust'

You might be faced with the situation where your employer has 'gone bust', in which case you may be unsure what your employment prospects are. It might mean your employer's company will be wound down and you will be made redundant. However, this is not always the case as the company might be acquired by new investors (see below).

Redundancy provisions only apply when a company has either gone into liquidation, receivership or an administrative order/ voluntary arrangement has been granted. If your employer has ceased to trade without any of these coming into effect it does not automatically mean you have the right to statutory redundancy payments.

## Transfer of business to new owners

Sometimes when a company stops trading because of insolvency problems it remains an attractive proposition to potential buyers who may indeed purchase the company and resume trading. Often it is a group of professional accountants acting as 'receivers' who decide whether the company is likely to attract a buyer and, if so, continue trading. If this is the case though, there is no guarantee that a new buyer will keep on all or indeed any of the staff. If the new owners do keep you on then they are normally obliged to honour the terms of your contract and any debts you are owed. If they do not keep you on you are not usually entitled to a redundancy payment unless it is as a result of reorganisation for technical or financial reasons. If you are dismissed as a result of a transfer and are not deemed to qualify for redundancy then you might be able to claim compensation for unfair dismissal or wrongful dismissal (see below).

Very often a company which has ceased trading for insolvency reasons will not attract a buyer and will go into liquidation. This means all its assets will be sold and the proceeds used to pay those individuals and organisations which it owes money to (called creditors). Since it is almost always the case that insufficient money is raised by the sale of assets to pay off everyone, the law lays down who has first call on any money available. The State also makes provision for paying redundancy in situations where there is a problem of this nature. This is explained in the next chapter in the section on statutory redundancy.

# Early retirement

This option usually comes up as part of a redundancy package whereby an employer offers early retirement in the form of pension payments. Obviously the amount of regular income the pension pays you will be scaled down to reflect the fact that you have started to draw earlier and contributions have ceased sooner than originally envisaged.

You need to determine whether you can live comfortably on the level of income this will provide both now and in the future. It may cause you to reappraise radically the lifestyle you had hoped to enjoy in retirement. More significantly you should be aware if you opt for early retirement and then obtain a job at a later date, the pension income on top of income from a job may push you into income tax or a higher tax bracket. Consider this very carefully and read Chapters 2 and 4.

# Termination and dismissal

In simple terms this heading deals with sacking. Your employer does have the right to sack or terminate your employment so long as certain statutory and contractual obligations are followed. These vary according to your individual circumstances and you should read the following carefully to see what is applicable to you.

If you have just been dismissed or are about to be it is very important that you obtain a copy of your contract if you do not already have one in your possession. The Employment Protection (Consolidation) Act 1978 requires employers to give their employees who work more than 16 hours per week a written contract which outlines their terms and conditions. This should be supplied to the employee within two months of their starting. Until recently the law was interpreted to mean that the only situation where you would be entitled to a written contract other than this is if you had worked for at least eight hours a week for five years for your employer. In March 1994 the House of Lords ruled that all 'part-time' workers (defined as less than 16 hours a week) had, in fact, only to work two years to gain protection.

The contract must include notice periods and disciplinary/grievance and appeal procedure.

## What if you never received a contract?

If your company has failed to produce a written contract there remain certain statutory rights which no contract can over-ride unless of course they are beneficial changes (for the employee). Employees are entitled to receive at least one week's notice after one year of employment, two weeks after two years and an additional week's notice for each year of employment up to a maximum of 12 years.

Furthermore, if it is the custom and practice of your employer to give terms more generous than those statutory rights referred to above you are able to argue that this was the case with your contract even though it was not in writing. Remember, there can be no doubt a contract existed: all that may be in doubt is what the arrangement was.

# Possible redress against your employer

There are two legal categories of dismissal whereby you might have redress against your ex-employer:

## (a) Unfair dismissal

If you have worked for your employer for more than two years you are known as a 'protected employee'. This means you are protected by law and as such have certain rights. If you believe your dismissal is unfair you have the right to take your case to an 'industrial tribunal'. This must be done within three months of your dismissal. Although two years' continuous service is usually the qualifying period to enable you to take the case to a tribunal, there is an exception. If you have been dismissed for trade-union activities then no qualifying period is necessary. Similarly, if you were dismissed because you refused to join a trade union then, again, you can go straight to a tribunal without the two years' continuous employment period.

An application to an industrial tribunal must be made within three months of the date of the alleged unfair dismissal or six months in the case of redundancy. There are two main parts to the statutory award which can be made by a tribunal. The first is a basic award element which is an amount of between £102.50 and £307.50 for each year of employment and the age of the employee. The second element of the award is compensatory and there is a maximum award of £10,000.

## (b) Wrongful dismissal

What about the employee who has worked for an employer for less than two years? What are their rights? If this is your situation then frankly you have practically no statutory rights. But do not despair, your rights are defined by the contract of employment which exists between you and your employer. That is why if you find yourself in this situation you should immediately obtain a copy of the contract and study it closely. If on reading this you decide that your employer has not followed the correct procedure or given you the required notice period, you may consider making a claim for 'wrongful dismissal' through the courts. Your solicitor will advise you how to formulate your claim for damages. The calculation of your claim will take into account the net value of your salary and other benefits that you would normally have been in receipt of for the period you would have been working had proper notice procedures been followed. There is, however, a duty on the employee to mitigate the employer's losses by attempting to find alternative employment as soon as possible. Obviously, if you have been allowed to work the notice period or been paid in lieu of notice then you cannot make such a claim.

The only situation where no notice is required is when there has been 'gross misconduct' (see below).

## What is 'constructive dismissal'?

Perhaps you are reading this book as a result of having resigned from your position in which case this section may be of relevance. If you resigned to pre-empt dismissal you may still have a case against your ex-employer. Quite simply, if your employer created a situation which did not follow the procedure defined in your contract and thereby placed you in a position where you were forced to resign, this is called 'constructive dismissal'. In other words, your employer 'constructed' your dismissal.

## Dismissal procedure

If you have just been dismissed or think you are about to be, check whether your company has a disciplinary/dismissal procedure. Your contract of employment will refer to this procedure and usually the actual detail of the company procedure is contained in a separate employee handbook which you will either have received when you started with your employer or alternatively is available upon request. Although each employer's procedure is likely to be different in the detail, the broad outline will follow common guidelines as recommended by ACAS. Listed below are the typical areas a disciplinary/dismissal procedure would follow:

- Verbal warnings
- Written warnings
- Dismissal.

### (a) Verbal warnings

These are sometimes known as a 'formal verbal warning'. This will normally follow a couple of informal conversations about the alleged problem. The purpose of the formal verbal warning is to record for the satisfaction of both employer and employee precisely what the problem is, how the required standard may be reached, what that standard is and how long is allowed to reach it. The employer must provide all reasonable assistance if asked to do so by the employee. Sometimes a time limit is specified but it would not normally be expected to be less than one month, perhaps longer if the problem is behavioural. A formal report detailing the above should then be given to the employee and a copy is kept on the employee's personal file.

### (b) Written warnings

Stage two of the procedure occurs when the formal verbal warning has not had the desired effect. This time the employer issues the employee with a formal written warning. Again, as with the verbal warning, this should detail why the performance/ standard is unsatisfactory and should outline ways of improvement and offer any assistance. The time limit will again depend on the circumstances but at least one month would be the norm. The employee will be told of the consequences if there is a failure to reach the standards set within the time-scale. The consequences could include dismissal. All these points should be covered in the written warning which will be given to the employee and a copy kept on file by the employer. During this stage the employee is usually given the option of being accompanied by a colleague of their choice or union official. On the other hand, if an employee's performance has improved then the note of the verbal warning will be removed and the copy of written warning removed at a later date (usually one year).

### (c) Dismissal

The third and final stage is 'dismissal'. This occurs when the verbal and written warnings have not had the desired effect. A formal letter is issued outlining the reasons for dismissal. The dismissal stage is usually invoked immediately and without going through the first two stages in situations of gross misconduct (see below).

*Performance.* Your employer would take this action if it was felt your performance was not up to a standard they might reasonably expect. This same procedure would be followed as a result of 'misconduct' defined in the next section.

*Misconduct.* Your employer will usually define misconduct as conduct and behaviour which falls below established codes of conduct and behaviour. Usually these will be listed and will include the following: persistent swearing, refusal to co-operate, sexual harassment, defacing company property, consuming alcohol on employer's premises, failure to notify manager/supervisor of reasons for absence, breaking health and safety regulations. This list is not exhaustive and your employer will usually state that it feels free to add other forms of inappropriate behaviour to its list if necessary.

*Gross misconduct.* As the term suggests, this is conduct or behaviour which your employers regard as so bad as to allow them to dismiss you instantly. This can be done without notice of termination or payment in lieu of notice. Typical examples would include theft, fraud, malicious damage to property whether your employer's or another employee's, drunkenness at work, gross insubordination, fighting/assault, use of non-prescribed drugs, falsification of records, constant absenteeism, disclosure of confidential information to competitors, etc, conviction of offences which are incompatible with continued employment, flagrant disregard of health and safety regulations.

Usually, employees who are faced with alleged gross misconduct charges will be entitled to attend a hearing of the evidence and will be advised as to the action that will be taken within a few days of that hearing. It is usual to inform the employee in writing and especially so if there has been a decision to terminate the contract.

## If you have already been dismissed ... what to do

If you have already been dismissed and your employer's procedure has not been followed then you ought to consult a solicitor specialising in employment law. You may have a case against your employer for 'unfair' or 'wrongful' dismissal. Take a copy of your contract and any literature on company dismissal/disciplinary procedure along with you to the solicitor.

## If your employer has already started disciplinary procedure

If your employer has just informed you that you are on a disciplinary procedure, check whether your employer is going down the correct route. Make sure you understand precisely what is required of you. Ensure you receive copies of any formal records. If you are entitled to have another person of your choice with you consider this carefully, they could act as a witness for you in the future. Finally, consider speaking to your manager/supervisor 'off the record' and asking what he or she thinks you should be doing. They might say something like 'Frankly, I don't see that there's anything you can do to bring your performance up to a standard that the company is going to find acceptable'. If you are told something like that you know you have got to start looking for another job immediately. That is not to say you should not attempt to meet your employer's demands; it just means you have been 'tipped off' about the likely outcome.

## Voluntary unemployment

If you resign from a job this is deemed to be 'voluntary unemployment' and has an impact on the level of benefits you may be entitled to. If you choose to resign rather than be dismissed then you must ensure you obtain the agreement of the company that your resignation was due to their unhappiness with you. Failure to do that could mean you are penalised.

Dismissal for 'gross misconduct' is also deemed to be voluntary unemployment since your behaviour was under your control. You will therefore have the levels of benefits reduced for a period of time (see Chapter 2).

## Negotiating the best deal when leaving

If you are being dismissed you do have some cards you can play to increase your 'pay-off'. First, if you are in a situation where you consider you have been unfairly or wrongfully dismissed, the mere threat of your taking legal proceedings should make the company more inclined to take great care that it deals with your leaving in a proper manner. Employers do after all have to consider their image with clients and the morale of their work force. It would not look very good if their employment policies were seen to be less than above board. For this reason alone an employer is more likely to err on the side of generosity if settling such an agreement.

The claim for damages should relate to the net salary and other benefits you would normally have been in receipt of during the period of notice you should have been given. Benefits relate to matters such as group life cover, medical insurance, company car, mortgage subsidy, meal allowance, etc. Also you can include a claim in respect of any commission or annual bonus which you believe may have become due in the period of notice you were not allowed to work. Remember, this is only a claim and you should not necessarily expect to get all of it.

This next point might seem rather a strange one but you should be aware that you have a legal obligation to mitigate (reduce) the potential claim on your ex-employer by getting another job as soon as possible. In other words, if your employer sacked you on the spot without giving you (say) the three months' notice required in your contract, then although you could submit a claim for three months' salary and benefits you must attempt to get a job to reduce this liability to you. If you did get a job then the income you receive would reduce the amount of money you can claim by the sum you were in receipt of in the notice period. All you need to do to satisfy the court that you have indeed attempted to mitigate your employer's loss is show evidence of job applications.

What other cards can you play with regard to your ex-employer? They might wish certain of their affairs to remain confidential from competitors. It might be acceptable to you to agree to certain clauses relating to poaching of clients or working for competitors.

Check what the situation is with regard to your pension: it may be possible to have a more generous lump sum transferred into your own pension plan. Group life cover normally costs the company much less per individual than it would cost you to provide the same level of cover. Since companies usually renew these annually it will not cost them any more to carry you to the next renewal. The same applies to other types of cover, and medical, dental and eye tests. Do not forget the company car: are they open to offers? If the car has been written down in the company's books it might represent good value to you if it is included in your package at that price.

One other benefit of increasing importance are employee share-option schemes. Your rights to these usually lapse on dismissal but there is usually sufficient flexibility for these schemes to be extended past dismissal. This could be very beneficial particularly if the shares are currently depressed. With predictions of stock-market increases they could become very valuable.

In negotiations do not overlook the value of a good reference being agreed. It is quite usual that an employer, as part of the final negotiation settlement, agrees to provide good written and verbal references.

Finally, be aware that the deal you conclude with your ex-employer could impact on the State benefits to which you may be entitled. Read the next chapter carefully. This applies not only to those facing unemployment and redundancy but also to those thinking about early retirement.

## Contacts

Advisory Conciliation &
Arbitration Service (ACAS)
Clifton House
83–117 Euston Road
London NW1 2RB
Tel: 071-396 5100

Commission for Racial
Equality (CRE)
Elliot House
10–12 Allington Street
London SW1E 5EH
Tel: 071-828 7022

Equal Opportunities
Commission
Overseas House
Quay Street
Manchester M3 3HN
Tel: 061-833 9244

Trades Union Congress (TUC)
Congress House
22–28 Great Russell Street
London WC1B 3LS
Tel: 071-636 4030

## Read

*Putting Redundancy Behind You* (Kogan Page) 1993

# 2
# A Guide to State Benefits
# (Some help through the maze)

This is a difficult area and obviously varies from individual to individual. That said, we have tried to present the information in a manner which is readily understood and allows you to get some idea of the benefits available and if they apply to you. *If you have not yet finalised the terms of your financial settlement with your employer then this chapter is very important.* If it is early retirement or redundancy which you are considering then this information should allow you to shape any settlement in a manner which takes account of its impact on your entitlement to State benefits and the correcting action you might therefore need to consider.

This book is concerned with employment and consequently the benefits we have focused on relate to this area. We have not focused on those benefits not directly related to this field although we have thought it prudent to mention them in case they have a relevance to your own circumstances. The benefits we have covered in some detail are the ones which will relate to the vast majority of readers.

This chapter divides benefits into:

1. Unemployment Benefit
2. Income Support
3. Sickness and Invalidity Benefits
4. Statutory redundancy
5. State help for getting back to work
6. Other State benefits in brief
7. Proposed future changes.

## Unemployment Benefit

Unemployment Benefit is paid by the Department of Employment to individuals who are registered unemployed and have sufficient National Insurance (NI) contributions credited in the last two years to qualify. If you supply your local employment centre with your NI number they will be able to determine precisely the level of your NI contributions. Alternatively you can write to the Department of

Social Security (DSS) at the Central Office, Newcastle upon Tyne or dial Freeline Social Security 0800 666555 for general information. If it is the case that you have made sufficient NI contributions during your period of employment and you are available for work, then you will qualify for Unemployment Benefit. If you have not made sufficient NI contributions then you probably qualify for Income Support (see below).

Unemployment Benefit is only paid for a limited period of a maximum of one year. After that period if your spouse is not working or working less than 16 hours you might qualify for Income Support.

## Backdating Unemployment Benefit

It is possible to backdate a claim for Unemployment Benefit by completing form UBL951. However, you will be required to state why you did not claim sooner. You will also be asked to explain what you were doing to find work by providing details of job interviews. The claim may be disallowed.

## The importance of claiming benefit

Some people made unemployed feel that 'signing on' is beneath them. First of all, remember, if you have been paying your taxes and contributing to the 'Welfare State' this is your entitlement. Secondly and perhaps more importantly, it is essential that your NI contributions are maintained as any failure to do so will affect many other State benefits including State pensions. If you sign on, these NI contributions will be maintained and benefits protected. The alternative is for you to fund NI contributions yourself, not a sensible option.

## Pensions and their relationship to Unemployment Benefit

If you are in receipt of monies from either an occupational or personal pension you should be aware that this pension income could reduce the amount of Unemployment Benefit you receive. This applies if you are over 55 years of age and are receiving more than £35 per week (before tax) from your pension. If this is the case your total Unemployment Benefit is reduced by 10 pence for every 10 pence your pension income is above £35. Sometimes when people retire a lump-sum payment is made from the pension scheme. This does not count as part of pension income since it is not intended to be payable over a specific period of time and is usually paid as an addition to an occupational pension. If you are in receipt of periodical redundancy payments which have been made as separate arrangements to your pension agreement these do not count as pension income.

It is possible that your personal pension income is at a level which only just stops you from qualifying for Unemployment Benefit, in which case it is possible you may qualify at a later date. This would occur if Unemployment Benefit rates are increased, you start claiming for a dependant, your pension income is reduced or stopped, or the £35 per week rule is increased.

## What if Unemployment Benefit is stopped by pension income?

The best course of action is dependent upon age. For men and women aged between 55 and 59 you will need to decide whether to continue signing on as unemployed. As mentioned previously, this has important implications in terms of NI contributions which count towards your State pension. If you continue to sign on you will usually get an NI contribution credit for each complete calendar week for which you are registered as unemployed. These will safeguard not only future State pension rights but also your future entitlement to Sickness Benefit and Unemployment Benefit. This could be important if for any reason your present pension income were to cease or be significantly reduced before the statutory retirement age. You should also be aware that credits are not given to women in the tax year in which they reach 60 or to men in the tax year in which they reach 65.

## What is the period of interruption of employment?

The period of interruption of employment (known as PIE) is the situation where you cease signing on but your circumstances are recorded. This means that if in the future you claimed for Sickness Benefit your entitlement is calculated on the tax year's NI contribution record that was used for your Unemployment Benefit claim. Depending on your past employment circumstances this may be more favourable to you than using later years' contributions paid while unemployed. It would also mean you would not have to serve the three non-payable waiting days.

If you are a male aged between 60 and 65 it is possible that the Employment Centre will advise you to follow the PIE course of action and stop signing on. If you are receiving Income Support this will not be an option. If you do follow PIE you will not be required to sign on and NI contributions will be automatically credited to you until you reach the statutory retirement age or any time up to the age of 70.

## When will PIE stop?

Apart from reaching retirement age as outlined above, PIE would cease if you started work again for an employer or on a self-employed basis for a period in excess of eight weeks. It would start again if you claim Unemployment Benefit after this period of employment.

### The effect of future changes to retirement age for women

In the November 1993 Budget the Chancellor announced that the retirement age for women qualifying for State pension was to be changed from 60 to 65. The changes will not affect any female over the age of 44 and means those under 44 will have to work longer.

## Income Support

In addition to Unemployment Benefit the Department of Social Security pays Income Support. The forms for claiming this will be issued to you when you go for your first interview at the employment centre. Even if you are not entitled to Unemployment Benefit you may be entitled to Income Support. If you do qualify for Unemployment Benefit it is quite possible you will qualify for Income Support as well.

Unlike Unemployment Benefit, Income Support is 'means tested'. In other words, the DSS will look at your outgoings and then work out the money you are eligible for. It is not a fixed sum as with Unemployment Benefit. They will take into account such matters as the number of dependent children and the amount of mortgage you pay. It is possible they will pay 50 per cent of the mortgage interest for the first 16 weeks and 100 per cent thereafter. You should be aware that the amount of savings you have can influence dramatically the amount you may receive from the DSS. Savings of less than £3000 will probably make no difference; savings of between £3000 and £8000 will cause a reduction in Income Support paid; and savings in excess of £8000 will probably render you ineligible for any Income Support.

To get Income Support you must be available for work and be able to show you are doing your best to get a job. However, if you are sick, a single parent or over 60 this may not be necessary. If you are a recent school-leaver aged 16–17 you will only get Income Support if you have to live away from your parents of if there are special circumstances such as being a single parent or registered disabled. You may qualify if you can demonstrate that the alternative is severe hardship.

## How is Income Support calculated?

There are three elements to Income Support:

- *Personal allowance.* This is a sum you are entitled to, a sum for your partner and a sum for any child you or your partner look after.
- *Premiums.* These are set sums paid for special needs, such as families, disabilities and pensioners.
- *Housing costs.* These are payments for housing costs, such as mortgage interest, and they vary according to circumstances. For the first 16 weeks you have signed on Income Support pay 50 per cent of the interest element of the mortgage. After this they pay 100 per cent of the interest element. If you pay rent you may make a claim for Housing Benefit. The forms for Housing Benefit will be supplied to you at the employment centre or by the DSS.

## The effect of redundancy payments on Income Support

When calculating the amount of Income Support to which you are entitled, the DSS will not only look at savings but also the terms of any redundancy payments. It does not matter if the redundancy package has been used by you to clear any outstanding debts, the assessment is made on the lump-sum payment you received. There is no point in paying off a credit-card debt or a car loan if the sole purpose was an attempt to reduce the capital cut-off points referred to above.

## The effect of voluntary unemployment on Income Support

Voluntary unemployment is defined as a situation where your unemployment has been caused by circumstances under your control. There are two situations which are commonly associated with this definition: if you have left your job without good reason or you have been dismissed for gross misconduct. If this is the case, your Income Support may be reduced for up to 26 weeks.

## Community Charge and Council Tax

If you are paying either of these, ring your local council to establish what you owed up to the point your employment ceased. Obtain a form (currently CCB1) to determine what rebate you will be entitled to.

# Sickness and Invalidity Benefits

Sickness Benefit will continue to be paid until April 1995 when it is proposed to merge it with the current Invalidity Benefit to create a new Incapacity Benefit. The details have not been finalised but it is proposed that the new benefit will be taxable.

The current Sickness Benefit should not be confused with Statutory Sick Pay which is paid while you are in employment. Sickness Benefit can be paid while you are employed *and during a period of unemployment*. To qualify for Sickness Benefit you must have made sufficient full-rate Class 1 NI contributions (Class 2 if self-employed). If you are registered unemployed and wish to claim Sickness Benefit you need to obtain form SC1 from your doctor or from a hospital. Fill this in as quickly as you can and send it to your local DSS office.

Sickness Benefit is paid for 28 weeks only but after that if you are still unable to be available for work you can switch to Invalidity Benefit. Invalidity Benefit is paid as long as your illness lasts but stops at the age of 60 for women and 65 for men. It can only be paid on production of a doctor's certificate stating that the person is 'incapable of work by reason of some specific disease or bodily or mental disablement'. It is made up of four parts:

- *Basic invalidity pension.* A fixed-sum payment.
- *Additional invalidity pension.* This is a sum based on your past earnings on which you paid Class 1 NI contributions. Obviously if your past earnings have been very little then you will not get much.
- *Invalidity allowance.* This is paid on top of the basic invalidity pension if you first became sick before you reached the age of 55 (women) and 60 (men). The amount varies depending on the exact age you were when you first became sick.
- *Dependants' benefit.* There is an additional benefit paid in respect of your dependants.

Finally, if you find you do not qualify for Sickness Benefit or Invalidity Benefit because your NI contributions have been too low, do not despair. If you are over 16 years of age you will probably qualify for Severe Disablement Allowance (SDA). To claim SDA you need to fill in the form which comes with leaflet NI 252 and return it to the local office of the DSS. The amount to which you are entitled will depend on the age when you became incapable for work.

# Statutory redundancy

Statutory redundancy is only paid to you if you are made redundant and have worked for your employer for more than two years since the age of 18 for at least 16 hours a week. In March 1994 the House of Lords ruled that the previous interpretation of the law contravened European law and statutory redundancy is now deemed to extend to part-time workers who have worked for an employer for two years. It follows that you must be over 18 years old. Furthermore, you must be under 60 (65 for a man).

## The payment you are entitled to

The amount you will be paid will vary according to what your pay was, how old you are and your length of service. You are normally entitled to a payment which will comprise the following elements:

- redundancy payment
- payment for any outstanding wages
- payment for holidays worked but not taken
- payment in lieu of notice.

These payments are normally made automatically.

## If you receive no payment from your employer

If you do not receive any payment you should contact your ex-employer immediately and put it in writing. You have six months in which to follow up non-payment but we would not advise you to take that long to pursue it. If you hear nothing and can demonstrate you have made attempts to get in touch with your ex-employer and no payment has been forthcoming, visit the Employment Centre. They will advise you whether you can make a claim on form RP 21.

## If your employer has become insolvent

If your ex-employer is insolvent you can make a claim for the unpaid wages, unpaid worked holidays, commissions, overtime, etc. The claim is made against the insolvency practitioner who has been appointed to look after the company's affairs. However, it is likely that you will not recover the full amount that is owing to you. There are limits to what you can claim which are reviewed every year and will depend on your circumstances. You may also be entitled to a compensatory award for failure to give notice. A compensatory award varies and is applied in the same manner as a court awarding damages. The award should compensate you for any actual loss you suffered. However, you are obliged to reduce the debt to you by seeking alternative employment or claiming the State benefits to which you are entitled. The compensatory award, unlike the redundancy payment element, is paid net of basic-rate tax.

## Occupational pension schemes and an insolvent employer

If you have worked for an employer who is insolvent it is important you check the state of the company's contributions and establish whether payments have been made on your behalf. It is often the case that employers facing cash problems cease contributing to the company's pension scheme. If you find this is the case then you should ensure that the scheme's administrator applies to the insolvency practitioner looking after the company for payment of the contributions by the Department of Employment.

## Claiming for someone who has died

If you are the personal representative who is legally entitled to act on the deceased person's behalf, then you are able to pursue the claim.

## Going to an industrial tribunal

You can refer any aspect of the terms of your redundancy payment to an industrial tribunal. Make sure you take any action within six months of the date of your termination. You can obtain a form and an explanatory leaflet from an Employment Centre or contact ACAS.

# State help for getting back to work

There are a variety of measures aimed at providing assistance in obtaining a job. These are:

- Job Clubs
- Job seminars
- Restart courses
- Interview travel expenses
- Family Credit
- Child Care Allowance.

There are different criteria for each and we have detailed these under each heading.

## Job Clubs

These operate on the basis that getting a job is a job in itself. The Job Club is open to individuals who have been out of work for six months since research shows that job hunting declines with length of unemployment. You will be meeting other individuals who are in a similar situation to you and with whom you can share your concerns. There will be between 8 and 12 members in each Club. You will be encouraged to construct letters and CVs and have access to stamps, photocopying and newspapers. By setting targets Job Clubs have been remarkably successful. You will receive ongoing advice and help from Department of Employment staff.

## Job seminars

A job-search seminar is aimed at those individuals who have been searching for work for at least three months. The seminar is designed to give you basic advice about how to go about finding a job. Normally the seminar will last for two days or four half days. The Department of Employment will pay your fares there and back.

## Restart course

This is open to individuals who have been unemployed for six months or more. It is designed to help you review and analyse your current situation and then help you devise a plan for getting back to work. You will get advice on the range of in-work benefits open to you and full details of the training opportunities open to you. Your benefits will not be affected by attending the course and your fares or petrol will be paid.

## Interview travel expenses

If you have been unemployed for more than four weeks you may get your travel expenses paid. Check with your Employment Centre before you travel whether they are willing to pay. You will be asked to fill in form TSI. The Employer will be asked to confirm the appointment. There are a number of criteria which you need to meet to qualify. These relate to the distance involved, the amount the job pays and whether the job is full time. Ask at your Employment Centre for more details.

## Family Credit

This will be paid to you if you or your partner meet a number of criteria and is aimed at encouraging you to take a job which may provide an income lower than you need. To qualify, you or your partner need to work at least 24 hours a week and have at least one child under 16 (under 19 if in full-time education, up to and including A level or equivalent). You can claim if you are employed, self-employed, a couple or a lone parent with a child.

It is not a loan and does not have to be paid back. You do not have to be on a very low income nor have a very large family. If you qualify you will also get free NHS prescriptions, NHS dental treatment etc.

**Child Care Allowance**
From October 1994 the Government will pay a Child Care Allowance to those in receipt of Family Credit. The idea is to allow mothers to return to work.

# Other State benefits in brief

There is a range of benefits which are designed for special circumstances and are not usually directly related to employment issues but which may have a relevance to you. We have listed them here purely as a means of highlighting their existence. If you think they might relate to you follow them up with the DSS.

*Social Fund Payments include:*

- Maternity payments
- Funeral payments
- Cold-weather payments
- Community Care Grant
- Budgeting loans
- Crisis loans
- Settlement and resettlement loans and travel grants.

*Other benefits related to disablement:*
- Mobility Allowance
- Attendance Allowance
- Industrial Injuries Disablement Benefit
- Workmen's Compensation Supplement
- Industrial Injury Compensation
- War Disablement Pension
- Invalid Care Allowance.

*Pensions:*
- State pensions
- Widows' pensions.

For more information about these special-needs areas, ask your local DSS for the relevant leaflets.

# Recap

After reading the above you should have some idea of where you fit in. Bear in mind the following points:

- Unemployment Benefit is paid for 12 months only.

- The amount of Income Support paid depends on income and any savings including lump-sum redundancy. It can be paid to supplement Unemployment Benefit.
- If you are to receive a lump-sum payment from your employer consider having it paid as a contribution to your pension fund. This will ensure it does not count as 'savings' and deny you Income Support.
- Remember that if you take early retirement the pension income will possibly exclude you from some or all Income Support.
- Make sure you register unemployed as soon as you are able to. It is vital your NI contributions are maintained for pension and sickness purposes.
- If you are about to 'resign' from your job rather than be 'sacked', remember this might be deemed to be self-inflicted voluntary unemployment which may affect the level of Income Support you are paid.

## Proposed future changes

In the 1993 November Budget the Chancellor outlined a number of changes to benefits which will come into effect in the future. Some of the details have yet to be finalised. The following paragraphs give an overview of what has been announced.

It is proposed to introduce a *Jobseeker's Allowance* in April 1996. This will replace Unemployment Benefit and separate Income Support payments. Under the new system those individuals who have made sufficient National Insurance contributions will receive a personal allowance for six months; after that the allowance will be means tested. Those who have not made sufficient contributions will be eligible for the allowance on a means-tested basis. The allowance will continue to be paid for as long as it is needed. At the point of introduction there will be 'transitional protection' to protect those affected during the changeover. To ensure that there is a genuine attempt to find work the Jobseeker's Allowance is backed up by a 'Jobseeker's Agreement'. The recipients will need to show how they intend going about getting a job and then follow that course of action through.

Means testing will not stop everyone with savings from receiving the new allowance.

There are three proposals which are to be piloted before being considered for the whole country. These are:

*The Jobfinder's Grant.* This will give direct financial assistance to people who have been out of work for two years or more when they find a job. It will pay up to £200 and is aimed at helping with initial transport costs or new clothes.

*Extended Jobplan.* This will be piloted to see if the success of the existing Jobplan Course can be built upon. It is proposed to introduce a new four-week course and provide help for young people aged between 18 to 25 who have been out of work for more than a year.

*Assigning caseworkers.* The idea is that young people aged between 18 to 25 who are unemployed for over a year will be allocated their own 'caseworker'.

## Contacts
Jobcentre/Employment Benefit Offices
Consult local Yellow Pages

Department of Social Security (DSS)
Central Office
Newcastle upon Tyne
Tel: 0800 666555
or consult Yellow Pages

Disability Advisory Service
Contact your local Jobcentre

# 3
# Your Financial Situation – Taking Action

It is possible that your unemployment or redundancy has come 'out of the blue' or that perhaps you had an inkling. Either way, when the day comes it is still a shock. Slowly the realisation of what has happened and the financial consequences sink in. Different people react in different ways but there is only one correct way to respond. You must face up to the situation and take whatever action may be necessary. Unless you are absolutely certain of receiving a regular income at a level on which you can survive you must conserve your financial resources no matter how large they seem. They can easily be whittled away. We have therefore divided this chapter into four main sections which effectively constitute an *immediate action plan for* coping with your changed circumstances within *the first few days.*

## Signing on

Having read the previous chapter, ring up your jobcentre/employment centre and ask for an appointment. At the appointment you will be asked to sign some simple documents for which you will need your NI number. The meeting will probably take less than half an hour and you will be given literature explaining the procedure. Although job and employment centres are part of the Department of Employment they will also have stocks of Department of Social Security forms which you can fill in to claim for benefits like Income Support. You will get some indication of what benefit income you are entitled to. If you do not receive any such indication then put in a request direct to the Department of Social Security – they are legally obliged to reply.

Sign on even if you have had monies in lieu of notice and are not yet entitled to any benefits for the reasons we outlined in the previous chapter.

## Household and personal finances

You need to determine just what regular bills you face and what income you are likely to receive. Be pessimistic and allow for unexpected costs. Start by detailing all your outgoings:

- Mortgage/rent
- Council Tax
- Gas
- Electric
- Water rates
- Telephone
- Home insurance
- TV/video/satellite
- TV licence
- Shopping
- School expenses
- Personal (clothing, credit cards, loans, catalogues, life cover, personal pension, dentist, bank charges)
- Car costs (HP, tax, MOT, servicing, petrol)
- Birthdays
- Others.

When you have completed this, detail your sources of income. Don't panic: there will be a deficit. Your priorities have to be:

- Keeping your home
- Eating
- Stopping any repossessions.

## Priority creditors

With this in mind decide who your priority creditors are and then write to them telling them how much you think you can afford to pay. Do it early and not when you have gone into arrears. By taking the initiative you are putting the ball in their court. You will find they will treat you much more favourably than if you had just pretended the whole debt would somehow go away and had only responded when legal action had been threatened. Indeed there is a school of thought which argues that you, the debtor, should bombard the lender with updates on the situation. Most lenders will come to some sort of arrangement with you. However you must stick to any arrangement you make.

The same applies to the utility companies, electricity, water and gas. So long as you contact them early they will usually come to some arrangement with you.

## Cutting your bills

Next, given your circumstances, work out what can be cut or cut out completely. Can your food bill be re-examined? Perhaps

Kwik-Save or Aldi should become your supermarket rather than Tesco or Sainsbury's. Look at your HP and credit cards: do you have any money which you can use to pay them off? There is not much point having some money in a building society account earning 6 per cent if you have a credit-card debt of a similar sum on which you are paying 20 per cent interest. Did you take any unemployment/redundancy insurance cover on your card?

Look at the amount you pay on your telephone. Do you rent one of your phones? If so do you need more than one? Can a member of your family lend you a phone? How important is the phone? There is a scheme whereby BT adapt your line to receiving calls only (except for making 999 calls). This option might not be practical if you are job hunting. There is another scheme whereby rental charges are cut in return for restricting the times you can make a call. However, if you do make a call outside the agreed times you pay heavy penalties.

If the worst comes to the worst and your creditors take you to court the fact that you have made offers to pay what you can afford will be taken into account. All your communications with the creditor should therefore demonstrate precisely this. A creditor who has failed to respond to these offers is unlikely to receive a favourable response from the court. Be sure, however, you stick to any arrangements you make.

There is one cost you might have to increase: life insurance. If you have been unsuccessful in getting your ex-employer to keep any group cover in place then it might be sensible to arrange some level of cover.

## Taking legal advice

If your leaving your ex-employer has been friendly and part of a general redundancy programme involving other employees, then this is not likely to affect you. If on the other hand you have read the first chapter and decide there were circumstances concerning your dismissal which you felt unhappy about, then you need to take immediate legal advice. Do not be concerned at this point about legal fees. Given your situation it is likely that any action you bring will be supported by Legal Aid and should therefore not cause you any costs. To make an appointment use your Yellow Pages to find local practices and then call them. Ask to speak to the partner who deals with employment law.

When you have made an appointment you must take along all relevant documents prior to your meeting. In fact it is a good idea to prepare a brief overview of the circumstances of the dismissal together with all relevant dates. Do not omit anything even if you think it damaging to you. Your solicitor will then give you his or her opinion on the merits of your case and the claim you might be entitled to make. Do not be afraid to question your solicitor closely and do not accept answers cloaked in legal jargon. Apply your own common sense in evaluating what the solicitor says.

If you decide to take legal action against your former employer it is important you apply for legal aid immediately. This will take between three and six weeks. The speed and scope of cover granted are factors which depend on your financial circumstances and the strength of your case. If you are registered as unemployed and in receipt of Income Support this is likely to facilitate the granting of your Legal Aid certificate. The Legal Aid board will merely contact your DSS to establish this is the case and, since Income Support is means tested, take this as ample proof you are without the means to pursue legal action with your own funds. As to the strength of your case this is determined by your solicitor who has to assess the strength of your case on a scale of 10–90 per cent.

## Holding on to your lump sum

It is with some degree of caution we mentioned the point about life insurance because if indeed you are fortunate enough to have received a lump-sum payment you will attract a life insurance salesperson's interest. The golden rule here is caution. You might need this money to live on; tying it up in an investment scheme could cause you a big cash-flow crisis. Many investment schemes have in-built penalties if you have to terminate them or withdraw cash from them within a certain time-scale.

You should keep your money in an account which is accessible and which pays a decent rate of interest. You can make your decisions as you start to adjust to your circumstances in the full knowledge your money is growing and is easily obtainable.

Also avoid the temptation to 'treat yourself'. Do not blow your money on holidays, rash purchases or by going out on the town. Keep it intact. Wait until you know your plan of action. Use the money to survive and then you can decide what to do with any money you may have left over. We have supplied further information on how to invest your money in the final chapter.

### Contacts
Citizens' Advice Bureau (CAB)
(Will provide some free legal advice and other services.)
Consult local Yellow Pages.

# 4
# Assessing Your Job Prospects

This chapter is about your worth in the job market. After reading it you may decide you have better options, perhaps early retirement, or starting your own business. Perhaps the only option is getting a job. Either way this chapter is designed to help you reach the decisions which are right for you. We have therefore divided this chapter into three main sections:

1. analysis of your employment capabilities
2. trends in recruitment
3. choosing the right job.

## Analysis of your employment capabilities

The first step is to take stock of what you can offer a prospective employer. In other words look at your marketability. Just what are your strengths and weaknesses? A marketing professional who wants to sell, say, a car or a packet of soap powder, will attempt to assess the situation. There is the product itself and there is the market in which it is competing. This exercise is known as a SWOT analysis: Strengths, Weaknesses, Opportunities, Threats. We suggest you undertake a SWOT analysis on yourself.

### The SWOT analysis
First take a sheet of paper and divide it into four columns running down the paper and equally spaced. In the first column write 'strengths', in the second 'weaknesses', in the third 'opportunities' and in the fourth 'threats'.

### Strengths
In the first column start to list those skills, qualities and experience you regard as positive attributes. Don't do yourself down and don't forget to include any experience gained from leisure activities or hobbies. Include any qualifications.

Perhaps the following examples would be helpful to you:

- Are you smart and tidy?
- Can you spell?
- Are you healthy?
- Do you have any formal qualifications?

- Do you drive?
- Are you good with people/old people/children/disabled?
- Do you speak another language?
- Can you do shorthand?
- Do you have keyboard/computer skills?
- Are you good with figures?
- Are you good at DIY?
- Are you a good organiser?
- Are you good at motivating?
- Have you good negotiating skills?
- Have you ever conducted training?
- Are you a good manager?
- Do you have good sales skills?

## Weaknesses

Head up the next column 'weaknesses' and list your failings. Be honest! The purpose of this exercise is not to depress you but to allow you to identify and tackle any weaknesses or, alternatively, rule out any occupations for which you are not suited. Examples might be as follows:

- No language skills.
- Hopeless with figures.
- Shy.
- Poor reading and writing ability.
- Terrified of computers/new technology.
- Can't drive.
- No experience of working with other people.
- Poor decision-making ability.
- Inarticulate/poor at expressing yourself.
- Poor time management.
- Bad general knowledge.
- Poor self-discipline.
- Poor self-image.
- Sloppy appearance.
- Poor telephone manner.
- Cannot map read.
- Bad accent.
- Difficulty in absorbing written information.
- Limited qualifications.
- Poor public-speaking ability.

## Opportunities and threats

The two columns you have now completed represent both 'opportunities' and 'threats' to your employment prospects. Head the remaining two columns accordingly and proceed to detail what action might be appropriate to maximise your opportunity or minimise a threat. Perhaps a couple of examples might be helpful.

You may have identified your lack of computer skills as a problem which could hold you back. This is clearly a threat and you should list it as such. However, it is also an opportunity which, if tackled, can be converted to a strength. It can be addressed by training which may well be an option offered as part of a government retraining package or at a local college of further education (see Chapter 5 on training). Alternatively, your lists of strengths may have identified a particular skill which you have gained from a hobby or leisure-based activity but which has applications in the job market. This is clearly an opportunity. For example, you may have been a home visitor for the church or WRVS and this may open opportunities in social-services work. Perhaps your knowledge of DIY would make you a possible candidate for a school or nursing-home caretaker.

## Using your SWOT analysis

Now you have identified your strengths and weaknesses and the opportunities and threats which follow, you need to be aware of the changes and trends in the job market. It's no use deciding to retrain for a trade that's in terminal decline. Match your SWOT analysis with what employers are going to need.

# Trends in recruitment

It is absolutely critical that before you undertake any training or embark on a new trade or profession you stop to think about the long-term prospects for you in that occupation. Of course this will not apply to everyone. After all, the priority may be to get any job which will pay an income. But if you are about to relocate or retrain be aware of the future trends and the effect they may have on your job security.

At the time of writing things may appear to look pretty bleak. However the fact is that not only will the recession end but also that employment patterns will change radically. In many respects both the UK and Europe will continue in the employment trends it has recently been following. Let us examine those trends.

First we need to recognise the profound changes that have taken place in the make-up of our workforce. You will probably have heard of the decline of Britain's traditional manufacturing base. During the 1980s this accelerated and saw the radical scaling down of 'heavy' industries such as ship-building, steel production, coal mining and the like. These kinds of industry once provided the bulk of the jobs in the UK. These jobs were known as 'blue collar' and were basically manual and required very little in the way of education or skills. Often sons would follow in their fathers' footsteps and whole communities would be dependent on a particular industry in the locality. All this has changed over the last few decades.

In the 1950s the leading research consultants, McKinsey, reported that of the UK's workforce over 70 per cent were employed in what could be termed manual jobs. Less than 30 per cent of the UK's workforce were termed 'knowledge workers'. This situation has, since 1950, begun to change, so much so that by the end of the century (not very far off now) the situation will be completely reversed. That is to say the requirement of the UK's employers will be a workforce comprising 70 per cent knowledge workers and a maximum of 30 per cent manual workers.

What do these continuing changes mean for the UK and the type of workforce which will evolve? Quite simply, the industries which are growing will require a more skilled and better-trained workforce than the UK has ever had before. At present the profile of skills represented in the workforce is inadequate to meet the demands of employers struggling to keep pace with technological changes and changes in the market-place.

There is one other major change which will have a significant impact on the nature of employment in the UK. The European Community entered a new phase with the introduction of the Single Market in 1993. The new European market has created new opportunities for the UK. Most of these will be in the service and finance industries.

So let us be clear, there will be a need for highly trained individuals. What about the likely 'supply' of individuals? This is where demographic factors come into play in a most critical manner. Demographics is simply the pattern of population in terms of growth and make-up. In short, the UK will have insufficient growth in its available working population to meet workforce requirements.

The situation is not confined to the UK but also applies to the European Community. Indeed, the situation facing the EC has been called 'Europe's demographic time-bomb'. It has been estimated that the European Community's available workforce will shrink by over eight million over the next 30 years. To put this in the context of the UK, the number of school-leavers will have halved by 1995. In other words there will be fewer and fewer individuals entering the job market and more and more entering retirement. Follow this through different professions and you will start to see the problem. For example, if every female school-leaver signed up to train as a nurse there would still be a shortage of nurses!

Think of another statistic. Remember we talked about a workforce being required by the year 2000 that was composed of 70 per cent knowledge workers? At present, only 18 per cent of school-leavers go on to higher education. So you can see the scale of the problem: the country will have jobs where seven out of every ten require specific skills and yet our education system will only be turning out two individuals out of every ten with qualifications.

Consider, too, the economic impact of the European Community's Single Market. The UK's economy is now part of a larger European one. Not so long ago the USA was the UK's biggest trading partner but not now. Germany alone is our biggest trading partner. Add the trade we do with the other ten member states of the EC and you can appreciate just how important this market is to us. Read the chapter on working abroad and the moves to standardise qualifications across the EC (Chapter 11) and you will start to appreciate just how significant Europe is going to be and the opportunities which will open up. Languages, particularly German, French and Spanish, will be increasingly valued. Remember, it will not just be a case of employment opportunities abroad but employment opportunities being created in the UK by EC member-state companies who might need bilingual workers.

What does all this mean? For employers it means ensuring they embark on training their own workforces, regarding their employees as a 'human resource' and protecting their assets from predators. Consequently if you are such a member, trained and qualified in your field, you should find that not only is your job security pretty solid but also that your employer will attempt to make your position even more 'locked in'. To this end many companies have started to look at the concept of flexible or cafeteria benefits. This system allows the employee to construct a benefits package from a list of options and so choose a benefits profile consistent with his or her profile. This sort of approach will be mirrored in other initiatives, perhaps the increasing introduction of crèche facilities to tempt qualified women back to work, or the introduction of flexible working arrangements to fit in with home life.

The only conclusion you can come to is that training is the key to job security. Not any old training but training in the expanding industries. For the first time in Britain's history, the government appears to have recognised the importance of practical training (ie, vocational training) and has reorganised the whole basis by the introduction of TECs and common, national vocational standards in terms of qualifications. Think long and hard about what the future is likely to mean in terms of your employment prospects.

## Choosing the right job

Your SWOT analysis will have identified your strengths and weaknesses, opportunities and threats. Match these against the current market trends in recruitment. From this you can assess the best course of action to take. It is probably worth pointing out that it is only really applicable to you if you want to acquire skills for a job that will last for some years to come. There will be little point in retraining and learning new skills if your priority is to get a job to last a couple of years until you retire.

If you have decided that your skills are out of date and you need to be retrained in order to get a job which will offer you greater long-term security, then this is the course you should follow. There has been much criticism of government money spent on retraining unemployed people in skills for which either there is no demand or where there is a massive surplus of skilled people in that trade. For example, what is the point of enrolling on a scheme to learn a trade as a brick-layer if all the evidence shows the construction industry is in decline and in the area you live there are hundreds of unemployed brick-layers?

The message of the last section is this. Push yourself to retrain in those areas where there is going to be a definite demand. If a five-year-old child can master the techniques of operating a computer, you can! Remember, ten years ago you probably thought a TV remote control was baffling new technology.

If you are career minded consult a career counsellor. The Department of Employment run job-review workshops which are two-day evaluation events involving a number of individuals in the same 'boat' as you. The workshop will provide you with a computerised analysis of opportunities and provide the necessary research into both career opportunities and training facilities. If you are interested in this, ask your local Jobcentre.

### Contacts
Employment Rehabilitation Service
Contact Jobcentre through Yellow Pages

Job Clubs
Contact Jobcentre through Yellow Pages

National Association for Care and Resettlement of Offenders
   (NACRO)
169 Clapham Road
London SW9 0PU
Tel: 071-582 6500

## Read

*The Mid-Career Action Guide* second edition (Kogan Page)
   1992

# 5
# Training Opportunities

So you've done the SWOT analysis, looked at the trends in the job market and decided training is a possibility you might consider. There is a vast array of options available, all of which depend upon your circumstances and background.

You should already have identified your weaknesses as part of your SWOT analysis and you should therefore be looking to undertake a course of studies or retraining which will plug that 'knowledge gap'. Only you can decide what your capabilities are, what time you can give, how much money you can spend and whether any training or qualifications should be specific to a particular industry/profession or more general in outlook. It is impossible to list every training possibility and qualification that may be open to you. However, the following headings should give you an idea of:

1. The types of qualification available
2. Finding training opportunities and method of learning
3. Financing your training and education
4. Training and Enterprise Councils (TECs) and Scottish Local Enterprise Companies (LECs).

## The types of qualification available

Broadly speaking, there are two types of qualification: general academic qualifications and practical work-related ones. There have been a lot of changes recently and we have therefore decided to list what qualifications are available and where they fit in.

### Academic

#### General Certificate of Secondary Education (GCSE)
These replaced the old 'O' levels (GCEs) and Certificates of Secondary Education (CSEs) and cover a massive range of different subjects. School students would normally take these examinations at 16 but obviously they are open to anyone of any age. These qualifications can be obtained by enrolling at a local college of further education for a period of study followed by examination. Enrolment is normally in September and lists of

colleges offering these qualifications can be obtained from the education department of your local council.

### 'A' level GCE

These are, quite simply, the 'advanced level' of the above qualification and they cover a wide range of academic subjects. These qualifications are the normal entry requirements of universities. As with GCSEs you can enrol at local colleges of further education and can study full or part time. You will have to enquire about the costs, which can vary, and ask whether there is a reduction for unemployed persons. It is possible to study 'A' levels by 'distance learning', as advertised in newspapers. The costs of distance learning may appear higher than enrolling locally. However, the correspondence course will contain all your literature requirements and involve no travel costs.

### Advanced Supplementary levels (A/S)

These fall in between GCSEs and 'A' level qualifications. The intention is to allow sixth-formers to have a broader education since the work load for each individual A/S is about half that of an 'A' level.

### Scottish Certificate of Education Higher Grades

Higher Grades apply to Scotland only and represent options for six-formers. Normally taken at 17, they are the standard entry requirement of Scottish universities.

## Vocational qualifications

There has been a significant increase in the amount of qualifications offered in recent years. In turn this has led to a reorganisation to ensure comparable standards exist across a wide range of industries and trades. The Business and Technology Education Council (in Scotland the Scottish Vocational Education Council) approve vocational courses and the examinations. The levels of qualification are as follows:

### First certificates and diplomas

These are aimed at school students who have been through the GCSE process and now need vocational training in a specific field.

### National certificates and diplomas (BTEC National)

These come after the first certificates and are more detailed and demanding. They are roughly equivalent to an 'A' level.

### Higher National Certificates and Diplomas (HNC/Ds)

Again more demanding than national certificates, requiring either an 'A' level or a BTEC National for entry on to the course.

With all the above the difference between a diploma and a certificate is (although the course-work is identical), a diploma covers more ground and more units are included in the examination.

### Certificate of Pre-Vocational Education (CPVE)
As the title suggests these are awarded for a course of study which comes before any vocational course-work. As such they are normally awarded to 17-year-olds who have stayed on an extra year at school.

### Technical and Vocational Education Initiative (TVE1)
This programme is intended to counter the criticism that the academic syllabus is unsuited to the demands of industry. The programme is therefore aimed at 14–16-year-olds who might need more practical education which will help them to gain employment.

### National Vocational Qualifications (NVQs)
These have been introduced as a means of determining what standard of performance has been achieved by a member of a workforce in respect to a particular job. These are now increasing in their scope and have gained acceptance in such industries as engineering, construction, agriculture, catering, hotel administration and retail sales. NVQs are a way people without formal qualifications can have their abilities and skills recognised formally and they duly receive a qualification.

## Higher education

### Degrees and HNDs
To get on a degree or HND course you will usually require good 'A' levels or BTEC qualifications. However, if you are an older (mature) student the entry requirements may be lower.

Degrees can be general or specific in their subject-matter. Many professions now demand a degree as a minimum entry requirement, eg the legal profession. An employer usually takes a degree whether specific or general at face value and regards its holder as having demonstrated evidence of ability to understand, absorb and analyse complex information. You should understand, therefore, that it is not necessary to pursue a degree in a particular subject in order to gain entry into some professions. To take the legal profession as an example, it is not necessary to obtain a degree in law. But it is useful. It has to be said that there is a growing demand from industry for degrees which do have some relevance to the chosen career. Consequently, many universities have reacted to this with the introduction of degrees which are much more vocational, eg 'broadcast journalism'.

### Postgraduate education

Following a degree it is possible to undertake further study either at a masters level or PhD (doctorate). Until fairly recently these further qualifications were really only for those who wanted an academic career. The 1980s saw the growth of the MBA: a masters degree in business administration. It has to be said, however, that not all employers seem to have accepted these as short-cuts to senior levels and consequently Britain at least has yet to see MBA holders achieve the success that might have been expected.

# Finding training opportunities and method of learning

If there are some courses or qualifications which you think are relevant to your needs you need to consider how you intend to study. The most common way is to enrol at a local college, university or whatever. However, it is possible to study by 'open learning' which we describe in more detail below.

## Training Access Points

Perhaps the best starting point is a visit to a local Training Access Point, usually found in libraries or colleges. These are computer terminals which allow you to scan the training courses and open-learning opportunities which are available to you in your locality. You can save yourself a lot of time and trouble by visiting one of these access points.

## The Open College

The Open College teaches by broadcasts on Channel 4 and special books. There is a wide range of practical subjects which you can study as a means of achieving a recognised qualification. Help and support are available to students through a network of local centres.

## The Open University

The Open University has been running for longer and is open to adults wanting to study for a degree. There are no entry requirements. However, there is a waiting list in many subjects which may frustrate your study plans. As with the Open College, the Open University broadcasts on the TV offer a range of supporting study material. The pace of study is largely left to the individual student and the course is very flexible. Students are normally expected to attend an annual residential summer school seminar usually held on a university campus.

## Distance learning

Distance learning is a more old-fashioned description of the open-learning process and is still used to describe those courses which can be undertaken on a correspondence basis. Usually the entire course comes to you through the post. You dictate when you study and the pace of study. Often the cost of the course appears expensive compared to direct enrolment. However, you should not forget there are no travel expenses and all the necessary work materials are usually provided.

# Financing your training and education

There are a number of ways of financing your training and education which depend on the course in question and your individual circumstances. There are basically three methods of financing:

- Free training at source
- Mandatory and discretionary awards
- Loans.

## Free training at source

By this we mean training or education provided 'free' and without any application for assistance. There are two broad categories included under this heading: those qualifications you enter while at school, such as GCSEs, etc, and those to which you can apply if you are registered unemployed (or in YT on leaving school), eg adult training. In other words, you have no involvement in the payment process other than enrolling.

## Mandatory and discretionary awards

The starting point in this complex area is to define the types of course which are eligible to receive mandatory grants. These are usually full time (including sandwich courses) and are in universities, publicly funded colleges and private colleges. The course of study should lead to a:

- University first degree
- Diploma of higher education
- HNC or diploma
- Postgraduate Certificate of Education.

There are some courses which, while not attracting a mandatory award, are eligible for a discretionary award. These include courses for teacher training and social workers. Basically, whether a discretionary grant is paid is down to the attitude of your local education authority (LEA).

## Postgraduate course grants

The main sources of postgraduate grants are the Science and Engineering Council and the Economic and Social Research Council. Other bodies which award grants are the Natural Environment Research Council and the British Academy. Your local university will provide you with details of these bodies and will also advise you of any grants awarded by local industrial sponsors.

Having established whether the course is eligible, the next question is whether you, individually, are eligible. The first criterion is whether you have been 'resident' in the UK for the three years before the start of the academic year in which the course begins (there are certain exceptions to this relating to work or study in the EC). The second factor concerns whether you have already been in receipt of a mandatory or discretionary grant. You would need to speak to your LEA to establish what their attitude is with regard to your own circumstances.

Although the main source of awards comes from LEAs, there are specific grants and bursaries available for certain categories of vocational courses. These include:

## Paramedical grants

For occupational therapy, physiotherapy, radiography, orthoptics, dental hygiene and dental therapy. These are awarded by the Department of Health, Central Office, Norcross, Blackpool, Lancashire FY5 3TA.

## Nursing bursaries

These are awarded as part of 'Project 2000' and they cover nursing education and various training courses. Contact your local health authority for further information.

## Sponsorships

Various bodies and organisations offer sponsorships for first degrees and BTECs. The Department of Employment publishes a booklet which details all this information. You can contact them at Department of Employment, Department CW, ISCO 5, The Paddock, Frizinghall, Bradford BD9 4HD.

# Loans

There are two types of loan:

- Student loans
- Career development loans.

## Student loans

Loans to students are paid out for the same types of course for which mandatory awards are available (see above). Loans that are government funded are meant to meet your living costs. There is a maximum which can be borrowed each year.

As with awards there are certain qualifying requirements which you must meet in order to be eligible for a student loan. The first is the residence requirement mentioned above. The second is you must be under 50 years of age when you start the course. Thirdly, you must have a bank account or building society account which has the facility to accept direct credits and pay direct debits.

The actual loans are handled by the Student Loans Company and you can only apply for a loan once you have started your course. The necessary forms are available from the place where you are registered to study. They will also endorse the forms to certify you are enrolled on the course.

You do not have to start repaying your loan until the April after you complete or leave your course. The sum outstanding will be index linked to the rate of inflation and so remain constant in terms of living standards. Repayments are made in a number of fixed monthly instalments. At present, this is 60 monthly payments for most borrowers but rising to 84 payments for those who borrowed for five-year academic courses. Repayments can be deferred if your income is considered too low.

## Career development loans

These are aimed at people who wish to undertake a vocational training course for which no free training is available. The loans are provided by the Department of Employment in conjunction with three high-street banks, the Co-op, Barclays and the Clydesdale.

Career development loans can cover up to 80 per cent of course fees plus the costs of books and materials. The minimum amount you can borrow is £300 and the maximum £5000. You do not have to be unemployed; the only qualification is that you must live or intend to train in the UK.

The loan covers most vocational courses and lasts at least a week but no more than a year. Nor must the course be financially supported by either an employer or by an award (grant).

No repayments are expected in the training period but must start within three months of the course ending. Payments are usually over a three- to five-year period. The exact term will have been agreed in advance. If you want more information about career development loans, you can obtain a free booklet by phoning 0800 585505, free of charge.

# Training and Enterprise Councils (TECs) and Local Enterprise Companies (LECs)

In England and Wales there are 82 TECs and in Scotland a further 22 Local Enterprise Companies (known as LECs), each covering a specific area. The intention is that each TEC will work with local companies to identify skills gaps and training needs. They have three main responsibilities:

- Training for new jobs
- Adding to existing skills
- Enterprise initiatives.

In this section we will look at those services provided by TECs and LECs which relate to training. We examine the non-training enterprise role of TECs and LECs in Chapter 10.

The great difficulty in detailing the services offered by TECs and LECs is the fact that each one will have arrived at different solutions relevant to the area in which they operate. What is common to all of them is that, having identified the training needs of their area, they will then have contracted a network of specialist training companies to provide that skills training.

Many TECs act as the co-ordinator of career/training assessment schemes or participate in such schemes. Since the TEC is in contact with local industry (in fact, its board comprises representatives from local industry), there is every reason to believe they have a good understanding of what local industry is looking for in a new employee. There are four main training areas:

## Youth Training

If you are 16 or 17 you are guaranteed a place on a YT scheme even if you are not unemployed. Above these ages you have to be unemployed and must finish the scheme by your twenty-fifth birthday. Youth Training can be provided by one of the specialist training companies (mentioned above), by employers, by local authorities and by further education colleges. The intention is that you gain a vocational qualification while training. This scheme therefore overcomes the criticisms of the old YTS, which often offered poor job experience with no qualifications at the end of it.

As we said each area organises itself differently, but the TEC will issue you with 'Training Credits' which can be 'spent' at approved training organisations. In the 1993 Budget the government announced that the Training Credits Scheme is to be expanded into a wider apprenticeship system in partnership with industry. It will aim to ensure there are some 15,000 apprenticeship places leading to NVQ (National Vocational Qualification) Grade 3.

## Employment Training

This is open to anyone aged between 18 and 59 and who has been unemployed for more than six months. There are priorities which are dictated by age bands, the length of time over six months you have been unemployed and the type of skill you want training in.

In addition to your normal State benefits you will receive an extra £10 a week. There may also be help towards travel, child care, lodging and any other costs associated with your training.

As with the YT scheme, training comes from a variety of sources and you can be certain that the training you obtain is both recognised and relevant. There could even be a job waiting at the end of your training. If there is not a recognised qualification at the end of your training, credits should be given towards obtaining one.

## Employment Action

This is similar to Adult Training in terms of eligibility and the benefits paid and this also provides temporary work. The intention is you maintain your skill levels in a period you would otherwise be unemployed. The average time of employment is six months.

The type of work varies considerably and could be on an individual basis helping in an administrative role or as part of a team engaged in a manual activity aimed at helping the community.

## Business Training

The TEC or LEC should make available a range of training courses aimed at providing you with the basics of setting up a business. Sometimes these are provided free and sometimes there is a small charge. For the other services the TECs and LECs offer in the field of enterprise, see Chapter 10.

## Contacts

Career Development Loans
Information from branches of Barclays, Co-op and Clydesdale Bank Branches, consult Yellow Pages.
Tel: Freephone 0800 585505

Careers & Occupational Information Centre (COIC)
Room W1108
Moorfoot
Sheffield S1 4PQ
Tel: 0742 594563/4
(Background information on different jobs and careers and sponsorship guide.)

Educational Counselling and Credit Transfer Service
    (ECCTIS 2000)
Fulton House
Jessop Avenue
Cheltenham
Gloucestershire
GL50 3SH
Tel: 0242 518724
(National database service to help you find out about higher and further education courses.)

Local education authority.
Look in your phone book under the name of your county, borough or metropolitan council.

National Council for Vocational Qualifications (NCVQ)
222 Euston Road
London NW1 2BZ

Open Learning
Room W1111
Moorfoot
Sheffield
S1 4PQ

Open University
PO Box 71
Walton Hall
Milton Keynes
MK7 6AG
Tel: 0908 653231

Training Access Points (TAPS)
St Mary's House
c/o Moorfoot
Sheffield
S1 4PQ
Tel: 0742 597344 for details of your local TAP

Training & Enterprise Councils (TECs) & Local Enterprise
   Companies (LECs).
Consult your local Yellow Pages or ring your Jobcentre.

University and College Admissions System (UCAS)
PO Box 28
Cheltenham
Gloucestershire
GL50 3SA
Tel: 0242 222444

# 6
# Setting Your Sights for Employment

If you have read through this book from the beginning you should by now know where you stand and what your prospects are. It may be you've decided you either want a job or want to change job. Perhaps you've decided on retraining as a serious option. Perhaps you're coming to the conclusion your age is against you and you will never work again. This chapter attempts to outline how you can organise yourself to achieve the objective you set yourself.

If it is a job you are after then we will look at how to present yourself through a CV and in the interview, where to find the job vacancies, constructing letters of introduction to potential employers and, if you are unemployed, how to organise your day. On the other hand, if you really feel you are unlikely to obtain employment again we have included a special section for you. We have organised the chapter under the following main headings:

1. The CV
2. Where to find jobs
3. Organising your day
4. The age barrier: some alternatives to getting a job.

## The CV

The purpose of the CV is to give your potential employer a summary of you. It need only contain those points that you consider relevant. It should contain no adverse or negative information. In short, it is an advertisement for you. It is therefore a very important document which your potential employer will possibly be going through line by line. It is likely to be the most important document you will write during your job search and it is worth taking time to construct it. You may need to 'play around' with the contents before you are happy with the final draft. Access to a computer or word processor is very useful in the context of this drafting process. However, it is not essential: it will just take longer without.

# CV basics

Here are some basic guidelines which you may find of use when constructing your CV. First, the objective of the CV is to obtain a job interview and this means you should not include any information which might cause your potential employer to throw your CV in the bin immediately. It should always include the following information:

- Full name.
- Address (including postcode).
- Telephone number.
- Academic qualifications.
- Vocational qualifications.
- Training apprenticeships undertaken.
- Work experience in chronological (date) order.

The above is the absolute minimum information your CV should contain, but you may wish to add information which you think is an advantage. For example, 'marital status' might be included if you think the potential employer sees marriage as a sign of 'stability'. Like it or not, some employers might see single parent or divorced as disagreeable. On the other hand, there might be circumstances where being single is an advantage, eg jobs with unsocial hours or perhaps abroad or requiring mobility. Sometimes an employer might regard young children as representing a problem. It is up to you to weigh these points up. Remember you are not obliged to give your race, religion or politics, but again these may be relevant at some stage of the selection process. Indeed, revealing this sort of information might be to your advantage. Many employers regard themselves as 'equal opportunity' employers and are keen to ensure their workforce reflects minority groups.

As you construct your CV refer back to your SWOT analysis (Chapter 4) and incorporate the strengths you identified. It is often a good idea to give a brief description of your duties and responsibilities for every past job you have held. For example, if you had held a job as a 'clerical officer' you might put down a summary which said: 'Responsible for dealing with customer telephone enquiries, constructing reply letters, filing all incoming documentation, preparing end-of-day cash balance', etc. For further ideas, see the sample CVs provided.

## Keep it short and precise

The length of the CV will depend on your background. However, we would recommend you keep your CV to a maximum of two sides A4 paper. If your CV fills only one side of A4 paper this is probably ideal. If it is in excess of two sides A4 you should attempt to rework it. Remember you will have an opportunity to expand on any of the items to your full satisfaction. If you find it difficult to get everything on two sides despite pruning, then try a smaller typeface or experiment with the format.

## References
It is quite common for some CV writers to include the names and addresses of their references. Don't! At this stage there is no need to give out this information since you have not been offered the job. Furthermore, your referees will become irritated if they find themselves inundated with requests from potential employers. Far better to say you will supply referees if this is necessary. If it does become necessary you can warn your referees that you anticipate a request from such-and-such an employer asking for a reference.

## Telling the truth!
A word about the truth and your CV. We have already mentioned that your CV is an advertisement and as such should not contain any damaging information. There is a question whether you should, to coin a phrase, be economical with the truth. It is clearly not only wrong to tell an outright lie but it is also dangerous. There is every chance you could be found out. One famous example was the poet John Betjeman, desperate to get a particular job as a prep schoolmaster. He lied about his skills at cricket, which was an important part of the schoolmaster's duties. Before his interview he 'mugged up' on the names of places on the cricket field and duly got the job. Only later was he discovered, but was kept on and given the worst team to coach.

Only you can decide on what to include and what to exclude. Common sense should guide. Slant your CV to give a positive image. If you were expelled from school, why mention it? If you failed some exams, do you have to highlight the fact? If you were sacked for bad performance, do you think a potential employer will be impressed? The rule is don't lie but do ensure you are selective. Also be creative. If there are gaps in your employment record, can these be represented more positively than just saying 'unemployed'?

## Customised CVs
If you have access to a computer it will be a relatively easy task to tailor your CV to the job for which you are applying. In other words, rather than having a standard CV which you despatch to each and every potential employer, you customise the CV to

ERIC MARK WAITES
11 Coogan Avenue
Rochdale
(061-532 5190)

STATUS: Married, two children

AGE: 38

EDUCATION:     Regal Comprehensive School, Harlow, Essex
6 O level passes, 3 A levels

Salford University
Business Finance Honours Degree (2:2)

EXPERIENCE:

1987–Present     ANTHONY HANLEY & COMPANY LTD
Manchester

*Media Planner Manager*

- Formulate media strategies and determine best plans for range of clients

- Presentations of media plans to clients

- Responsible for £500K media spend

- Supervision of Media Planning Team

1979–87     COOGAN MARKETING GROUP PLC
Birmingham

*Media Buyer*

- Negotiated rates for clients of the agency

- Placed adverts in local and national media and monitored response

- Contributed to the production of radio commercials

| | |
|---|---|
| Name: | **James Richard GRAY** |
| Address: | 27 Rosebury Grove<br>Splott<br>Cardiff |
| Telephone: | 0222 41787 |
| Date of birth: | 6/3/61 |
| Education: | Kingsley Grammar School, Surrey |
| | GCE O Levels: Maths, English, Biology, Geography, RE and History |
| | GCE A Levels: Economics, General Studies |

**Employment:**

**May 1989–to date** — **AUTO FIRST FINANCE LTD**
Bristol
*Corporate Loan Manager*
Responsibilities include supervision of four-person team of sales executives. Setting targets and ongoing monitoring. Submission of credit proposals to Head Office.

**June 1984 to April 1989** — **METROPOLITAN CREDIT PLC**
Cheltenham
i) *Senior Finance Executive*
Developed retail client base by regular contact. Worked to set objectives. Responsible for sales penetration and ongoing training of retail outlet staff.
ii) *Service Representative*
Assisting Finance Executives in the administration of the branch client base. Processing of finance documentation. Submission of credit data to Head Office for credit scoring.

**Sept 1979 to May 1984** — **MAXWELL BANK PLC**
Kingston
*Debt Collector*
Control of debt book, calling on debtors, preparing legal documentation. Compilation of monthly reports on debt ratio.

**Interests:** Swimming, fell walking and family pursuits. I am also a local Scout Leader.

Stephen Cecil Appleton
The Cherries
Jordan Avenue
Erdington, Birmingham
(021-888 9990)

| | |
|---|---|
| PERSONAL: | Single, born Southampton, July 1938 |
| EDUCATION: | Middlesex County School |
| QUALIFICATIONS: | School Certificate Passes in English, Maths, History and Geography.<br>HGV Licence (clean) |
| HEALTH: | Excellent |

WORK EXPERIENCE:

**4/1993–Present**    *ERDINGTON VOLUNTEER TRUST*
After redundancy I have combined attendance at my local Job Club with voluntary work for a local community organisation working on environmental projects. Duties include assisting in project planning and viability reports. Organising day shifts for volunteers. On-site team work.

**6/1977–4/93**    *MIDLAND FOOD CORPORATION*
Birmingham
i) *Transport Supervisor*
Responsible for co-ordination of drivers for Birmingham depot vans. Organisation of driver rosters and liaison with Food Distribution Department. Charged with ensuring vans were maintained to company standards and kept roadworthy. Liaison with Servicing Department.
ii) *Van Driver*
Part of the Birmingham Depot Distribution Van Fleet. Delivering food products to supermarket chains. Adherence to strict timetabling and scheduling. Maintenance of daily record logs. Responsible for maintaining vehicle to company standards.

**10/1968–6/1977**    *MOSELEY PRODUCTS LTD*
Tamworth
*Customer Deliveries Organiser*
Organised deliveries to national customer base. Acted as stand-by driver in addition to four-man delivery team. Liaison with Company Administration Department to co-ordinate delivery schedules.

| | |
|---|---|
| 4/1963–5/1968 | *GREEN & LITTLE LTD*<br>Cannock<br>*Security Guard*<br>Part of six-man team guarding factory premises. Worked on shift system. Commended for action resulting in arrest of burglars. |
| 10/1958–3/1963 | *BIRMINGHAM CONSTABULARY*<br>*Police Constable*<br>General policing duties, working with the public. Gave evidence in court. Routine administration duties associated with policing. |
| Interests: | Since my redundancy I have concentrated on my search for employment. In addition to my voluntary work I maintain a keen interest in sport. I enjoy jazz music and I am a member of CAMRA. |

---

JANE F. COLLINS
12 Sandy Road East
Windsor
(181-222-0000)

**Work Experience:**

| | |
|---|---|
| 1987–Present | LONGHURST SHIPPING CO<br>Liverpool<br>Technical Secretary<br>Handle word processing for Export Section. Compose correspondence and issue manifests. Maintain and organise client files and manifest logs. Record invoice details and quotation requests. |
| 1983–1987 | ELITE CHEMICALS LTD<br>Warrington<br>Bookkeeper<br>Organised daily ledger system. Monitored client account status and dealt with credit requests. Compilation of monthly invoicing and submission of reports to Accounts Manager. |
| Education | St Mary's High School, Leigh<br>6 O level passes in English Language; English Literature; History; RE; Maths and Art.<br>Form Captain in Fourth Year.<br>Member of School First Hockey Team. |
| Personal Details: | Born 1966, Runcorn, Cheshire.<br>Married, no children.<br>Clean driving licence. |

highlight those skills which have a particular relevance. You must remember to keep a copy of each 'customised' CV or you could well find yourself attending an interview without any idea of what it was you actually put in your CV. Needless to say, this could put you at a distinct disadvantage in the interview situation.

# Where to find jobs

Having constructed your CV you now need to start your job search. You might be surprised at the range of job sources available. Some of the information may be applicable to your particular circumstances. Having said that, most job seekers will find something relevant to them in the information detailed below. It should be stressed that this list of job sources is not exhaustive but it will give you some good ideas you can follow up.

## Employment Centres (formerly Jobcentres)

Great strides have been made in the past few years by Employment Centres, which have become user-friendly, 'one-stop' service centres. You will find a list of job vacancies displayed on large boards. You are free to browse at leisure. If there is a vacancy of interest to you a member of staff will assist you and possibly arrange an interview for you with the prospective employer. You will also find that Employment Centres are a mine of useful information about career opportunities. This may be in the form of literature, magazines and videos. It has to be said that the majority of vacancies at an Employment Centre will be for unskilled work, manual, junior administrative and commission-only sales jobs. All the Employment Centre services are provided free to both you and potential employers.

## Careers Offices

These are usually run by local education authority departments. You will find details of these in libraries and in Employment Centres. The careers offices have specialist career advisers and will give you details of the local jobs market.

## Employment agencies

These are privately run agencies and may be local or part of a national chain. Some of the more well known ones are Link, Wilmingtons, HMS, Brook Street, Alfred Marks and Reed. You will find that the bulk of positions these agencies handle will be clerical and secretarial. However in some cities they may have started to specialise in a particular industry, for example vacancies in export/import or computer-skilled staff or hotel staff. It is sometimes possible to get junior accountancy positions through these types of agency.

Sometimes these agencies will offer employers a supply of temporary staff. This simply means an employer will contact the agency if they require extra staff or a short-term replacement. The length of temporary work will depend on the circumstances. Some people enjoy 'temping' and prefer it to being in one permanent job. Moreover it is often a good door opener to full-time employment. Many 'temps' have so impressed their employers that they have been offered a full-time position.

It is important that you appreciate that many of the jobs the agency has on its books will not be advertised anywhere else. If an employer has been happy with the past service provided by the agency it is likely that they will start to use the agency on an ongoing basis. Consequently, when the employer has vacancies they will notify the agency and thereby avoid all the 'hassle' of having to wade through reams of applications which would almost certainly have been received in response to an advertisement. It is therefore very important that once you have registered with an agency you cultivate a relationship with them. You need to ensure that your name remains front of mind and is not consigned to the filing cabinet. Finally, you ought to know what is in all of this for the agency. Quite simply money, not from you (that is illegal) but from the employer who pays the agency a percentage of the first year's earnings. Of course, if no one is suitable and the employer finds an employee from elsewhere, then the agency gets no fee. All this area is a matter between the agency and the employer and need not concern you.

## Recruitment consultants

Recruitment consultants are more up-market versions of employment agencies. They differ inasmuch as the positions offered will be more senior and many of them more specialised. Since the positions will be nationwide, recruitment consultants will have only a limited number of office locations. They will therefore rely on advertising to ensure they reach the right people. From the response to those advertisements, the recruitment consultants will draw up a list of possible candidates they consider suitable for the job. At this stage the recruitment consultants might conduct the first round of interviews. They might pass on this short-list to their client or they might conduct the interview with the client also participating. The real function of the recruitment consultant is to ensure, through placing advertisements in appropriate places and by ensuring the correct form of words, that a good response is delivered and these are filtered down to a short-list.

It is possible to 'register' with a recruitment consultant so that you are on file and should therefore be considered for any suitable vacancy that comes up. If you have sent your details in for a specific advertised vacancy you can still ask that your details be kept on file for such an eventuality.

Recruitment consultants vary in their professionalism and it is quite surprising how incompetent many of them are. Do not be surprised or down hearted if many of them do not even have the courtesy to acknowledge receipt of your application. If you receive nothing back after a few weeks you can call or write again. If you have no joy you could always write to the recruitment consultants' clients (if named in the advertisement) pointing out in a polite manner what has occurred and whether they should be using such an unprofessional organisation.

You should also be aware that there are two basic differences in the organisational style of recruitment consultants. Usually a recruitment consultant advertises on behalf of a client for specific vacancies and is therefore genuinely 'recruiting'. The other method is to advertise 'vacancies' about which details are very vague. They succeed in attracting your interest. In reality these 'vacancies' do not exist and the intention is to stimulate a response from a wide range of people seeking a position. Once in receipt of these application forms, the recruitment consultant selects the applicants they consider the most interesting. They then proceed to canvass their industry contacts in the hope that their potential client will express an interest. This approach is often used by new recruitment consultants attempting to gain a reputation in a particular field.

It should be stressed that there is nothing wrong in this approach, it may get you a job. On the other hand, do not raise your hopes when you see what appears to be an ideal job vacancy which, in fact, does not exist.

A word about the payment procedure concerning recruitment consultants. As with employment agencies no payment is required from you, their payment is from their client if they are successful in placing a new employee. It will cost you nothing to register.

## Executive search consultants

Also known as 'headhunters'. These organisations operate on a much lower profile than either of the two outlined above. As such they do not often advertise, normally working by word of mouth and industry contacts. Through such networks they expect to know who the best candidates are. Very often search consultants are highly specialised and this is how they are able to know exactly what is happening in a particular job market. It is likely that there will be only a limited number of individuals capable of filling the vacancy and it is also likely that these individuals are not looking for a job change. It is therefore essential that any approaches are subtle and very discreet. The search consultant will probably have the authority to present an 'offer' which will at least entice the potential candidate into considering the prospect of a job change.

### A warning about search consultants

Now a word of warning. There are companies which, on the surface, appear to be 'search consultants' but, in reality, are not. They usually advertise in the jobs pages of the national daily newspapers. The adverts will begin with headlines like 'REDUNDANT – WANT A CHANGE?', 'EXECUTIVE... NEED A JOB?', 'OUT OF THE COUNT?' or 'REDUNDANT DIREC-TOR ... EARN £30, £40, £50, £60, £70, £80K!!!' They will also claim to have access to 'unadvertised' jobs. They will offer to give you 'tailored' analysis, give you confidence, help you secure the 'right' position.

Let's be clear what will happen if you respond to one of these advertisements. First you will be invited to an interview. At the interview you will be informed, 'yes', they can definitely help someone of your status. However, this will cost some money but they do take Barclaycard. This can be anything from £250 to £500. A few sessions coaching and you will probably have no problem getting a job perhaps from one of their 'contacts'. Whereas it is true to say that a very large proportion of jobs go unadvertised it is an entirely different matter to imply all these jobs are stored on some secretive database which only certain organisations have access to. It is up to you whether you think you would benefit from such an exercise and whether it is worth the expense. If money is tight we do not think it is. If on the other hand this option has been offered as part of a redundancy package and the service is free then, fair enough, you may consider you will get some benefit from it.

## Newspapers

As you will be aware, there is a wide variety of newspapers published on a local and national basis. Some will be daily, published in the morning, others in the evening. Others still will be weekly. Virtually all newspapers will carry recruitment advertising. Some local evening newspapers will only carry job vacancies on certain days. Thursday is the most common and you should check this out to avoid the unnecessary expense of buying the paper on evenings when no job vacancies are carried.

National newspapers vary in the number of jobs carried. However, *The Daily Telegraph* has a reputation for carrying the largest number of job vacancies of the national dailies in its Thursday edition. Having said that, the other quality dailies do try to specialise in certain professions on other days of the week. Rather than buy every quality paper every day you might find a trip to the library is the most cost-effective way.

The Sunday newspapers also carry recruitment advertising. Two Sunday newspapers dominate the situations vacant advertisements. *The Sunday Times* and *The Sunday Telegraph*. It should be noted, however, that *The Sunday Telegraph* jobs section is usually a reprint of the same advertisements which appeared in the previous Thursday's edition of *The Daily Telegraph*. You will also find some jobs advertised in the *Independent on Sunday* and *The Observer*, particularly those in the public sector.

Recent years have seen the development of regional job newspapers almost exclusively devoted to situations vacant. Very often these are owned by the regional evening papers and simply reprint all the job advertisements contained in their other regional newspapers. This can represent a very cost-effective way of ensuring you cover the wide geographical area without having to purchase a number of regional evening newspapers.

Local weekly newspapers are a good source for local jobs. If you are seeking a senior/executive position it is unlikely you will find suitable vacancies advertised in local papers. By all means use them, but look elsewhere as well.

## Trade press

If you are looking for a particular job in a specific trade or profession there will be a dedicated journal, magazine and newspaper which covers that particular area. If you are unsure what the relevant titles are you can find a full list of publications contained in various directories such as *Benns Media Directories*, *Willings Press Guide* and *British Rate and Date (BRAD)*. These are usually available in good public reference libraries. Copies of the magazines you require may also be available at the library. You may be surprised at just how specific some magazines are and it is imperative that you establish whether there is a trade magazine which is relevant to you and carries situations vacant. This could be the most important source of potential jobs.

## Local radio

Check out whether you live in an area where your local radio station advertises job opportunities. Usually this is done at a set time of the day on a regular basis. Usually, but not always, the kinds of job advertised are similar to those found in an Employment Centre.

## Teletext and Ceefax

If you have access to a TV with a teletext facility, you can use Teletext and Ceefax to check out job vacancies. The 'Jobfinder' service is more comprehensive, while the BBC's Ceefax page 696 only details jobs in the BBC for which they are recruiting. Teletext also gives details of training schemes which are available. These services are to be found on page 241. If you do not have a teletext facility, the 'Jobfinder' is broadcast at night time and you can either view then or video it.

## Factory noticeboards

This method of advertising job vacancies has declined over recent years. Some factories still advertise vacancies on noticeboards outside the factory gates. If you are seeking domestic work also check noticeboards in shop windows and in some supermarkets (Kwik-Save is one).

## Word of mouth

Do not forget friends who are in work as a source of potential jobs. They will often hear of vacancies before they are advertised. If you feel comfortable with this approach make a list of people to contact. Let them know that you are looking for employment. If appropriate, make a date to meet them socially and pick their brains for ideas. Ask them if they know of any opportunities. If they do find out how to follow it up. Is there a person to write to? Is it okay to mention your friend's name?

## Speculative enquiries

Read newspapers to keep in touch with what is going on in the particular trade/industry you wish to get a job in. Be sure you are abreast of issues which might have an impact on job prospects. Is a company expanding? Has a company relocated to your area? Has a company announced a change in the type of workforce it wants to employ, eg more part-timers? With this in mind use your Yellow Pages to draw up a target list of potential employers in your area and then write to ask if they have any vacancies in the field you wish to enter.

# Organising your day

So far you have constructed your CV and determined where you are going to get your job leads from. We now need to examine how you organise your day. It stands to reason that you should be using your free time to pursue a job but there is also another reason which demands you take the organisation of your day very seriously . . . morale.

Let us look at this problem of morale. From the outset you must realise that your period of unemployment is a battle: a battle to maintain your self-confidence, a battle to maintain your pride, a battle to maintain standards. Most people need a purpose in life and need to feel they are making a contribution. To win this battle you must set yourself standards and targets and then keep to them.

## 'Slobbing out'!

If you are not careful your period of unemployment will reduce you to a lazy slob who achieves nothing, becomes listless and truly redundant. What are the characteristics? We will list them to ensure you are aware of the first symptoms. A typical day might go something like this:

| | |
|---|---|
| 9.00–10.00 | Get up (later than you used to). Don't bother shaving/doing hair/make-up. Have breakfast, watch *Kilroy*. |
| 11.00 | Drink coffee, read the paper. |
| 11.30 | Get a shave/put make-up on. |
| 12.00 | Walk down to the local shops for cigarettes. |
| 12.10 | Back to watch *Rainbow* and have another cuppa. |
| 12.30–1.30 | *Neighbours* followed by news and bowl of soup. |
| 1.30–2.00 | Read newspaper again on loo. |
| 2.00 | Put telly on again, flick channels. |
| 2.30–4.00 | Watch corny black-and-white film. |
| 4.00 | Go to supermarket to buy litre container of milk/ pick up kids from school. Collect evening paper. |
| 4.30 | Back home for cuppa. |
| 5.00 | Watch *Blue Peter* with kids/read paper. |
| 6.00 | Evening meal. |
| 7.30 | Settle down for a snooze and watch telly or go out to the pub. |

Of course there are variations on this. Perhaps you take the children to school and get a newspaper, perhaps you 'nip down' to the pub for a lunch time drink? Whatever, the pattern is the same.

If you recognise any of these characteristics then you could be in trouble. You are not going to find a job if this is your typical day. More to the point, your morale and self-esteem will be non-existent. How then should a positive day begin? First you should behave as though you were still employed. Get up determined to follow through a series of goals. A suggested itinerary might be as follows:

| | |
|---|---|
| 7.30 | Get up, wash, etc, dress smartly. |
| 8.00 | Breakfast. |
| 8.30 | Leave house to go to reference library. |
| 9.00 | Research career opportunities, read journals and trade magazines, newspapers. Call at job centre. |
| 12.30–1.30 | Lunch, watch news. |
| 1.30–3.00 | Draft CVs, letters, etc. |
| 3.00–4.00 | Carry out some worthwhile study, eg learning a language. |
| 4.00–5.00 | Call employment agencies. |

## The age barrier: some alternatives to getting a job

Of course most of the above is only relevant if you really are looking for a job. If you are 55 years old and have resigned yourself to the fact that you will never get a job, then make that your starting point. Instead you should consider other alternatives which will stop you wasting your time. These are:

- setting up your own business
- voluntary employment
- living abroad
- pursuing an interest.

There is a separate chapter (Chapter 10) on setting up your own business, so we will not cover that here.

### Voluntary employment

If you are unemployed there is nothing to stop you undertaking voluntary employment. So long as you remain available for work and could start at 24-hours notice, your benefits will remain unaffected. The other criteria are you must not receive any pay and you continue to look for work.

Voluntary work encompasses a wide range of possibilities. It could, for example, mean working with the social services department. Perhaps there is a charity you would like to work for?

What about the local hospice? Working there might put things into perspective. If you have skills and are willing there is a whole host of organisations desperate for help. It may not be what you are used to but the reward of contributing something useful to the community is certainly available.

## Living abroad

This is the subject of Chapter 11. The purpose of its inclusion at this stage is to draw it to your attention as an option to consider. It is often cheaper to live abroad. If your sole intention is to survive on a small pension until your State pension starts, this may be an option. EC member states such as Spain and Portugal are possible options. If your concern is language and culture, consider Cyprus. They speak English, drive on the same side, have the same legal system, have the same electricity system. There are British military bases and you can receive some British TV programmes. There is even a Marks & Spencer. In short, do not dismiss living abroad out of hand.

## Pursuing an interest

If you have long had an interest, why not take this opportunity to pursue it? Use your time constructively. Develop new interests and set yourself targets. Have you considered learning a language? Are there any relevant TV and radio programmes which tie in? Are there any subjects which you could write a book about? Are there any interests you could pursue which, although costing some money to start, might actually save money? Have you considered growing vegetables in your garden? For a few pounds you can start home wine-making. Finally, what about turning your hand to practical matters, making things like bird tables or wooden toys for your grandchildren?

## Contacts

British Trust for Conservation Volunteers (BTCV)
36 St Mary's Street
Wallingford
Oxfordshire
OX10 0EU
Tel: 0491 839766
(Organises a wide range of conservation projects needing volunteer input, can arrange accommodation on some projects.)

The Central Bureau
Seymour Mews House
Seymour Mews
London W1H 9PE
Tel: 071-486 5101
(Produces a guide on volunteer work.)

Community Service Volunteers (CSV)
237 Pentonville Road
London N1 9NJ
Tel: 071-278 6601
(Need volunteers for temporary placements on community service, no qualifications needed.)

International Voluntary Service (IVS)
162 Upper New Walk
Leicester LE1 7QA
Tel: 0533 549430
(Organise international voluntary projects based in camps for people aged between 16 and 60. Projects can be for a few weeks to two years.)

Recruitment and employment agencies
Consult your local Yellow Pages.

## Read

*How You Can Get That Job: Application Forms and Letters Made Easy* (Kogan Page) 1992
*Job Hunting Made Easy* 2nd edition (Kogan Page) 1992
*Preparing Your Own CV* (Kogan Page) 1990

# 7
# Preparing for an Interview

## The purpose of an interview

As a starting point let's examine what the purpose of an interview is. From a potential employer's point of view, this is an opportunity to establish whether you are willing and capable of filling the vacancy which is on offer. To have gained an interview you will have already convinced your potential employer through your CV that you have some relevant qualities and/or skills. What a CV cannot do is demonstrate what you as a person are like. What kind of personality are you? Are you confident? How do you react to a line of questioning? Do you have a genuine level of knowledge to back up the claims you have made on your CV? Employers will want to establish whether you will 'fit in' with other employees and the culture of the organisation. Are you a 'team player'? They may need to establish whether you can express yourself logically or how you might react under pressure. Obviously, the type of concerns an employer will have will depend on the type of job you have applied for.

To give some examples, if you are a computer programmer with a high level of technical knowledge that requires little contact with other employees or clients/customers, it might not matter if you come across as a shy and tongue-tied individual. On the other hand, if the position for which you have applied involves working with other employees and the general public the employer is not likely to select an individual who is, say, morose, shy, 'prickly' or just downright short-tempered and rude. In the section below we will examine how you should prepare yourself for the interview by, among other things, anticipating what qualities the employer is looking for.

You might expect companies to take interviewing very seriously since the consequences of failing to select the right candidate can be very costly. It is therefore very surprising that a number of companies allow interviews to be conducted by employees with no training in interview techniques. It is quite often the case that the interviewer might be made more nervous about the whole interview process than you are.

# Preparation

## Background to the position

Sit down with a pad of paper and the original advertisement which details the job vacancy for which you are applying. What qualities are they going to be looking for above and beyond qualifications? Some examples might help you. If you have applied for a salesperson's position which involves working under your own supervision it is certain one of the employer's major concerns will be to identify whether you have sufficient self-discipline. Are you what is known as a good 'self-starter'? If the job you have applied for is 'Customer Relations Officer', what kind of personality will they be looking for? You can bet it will not be a crabby cynic with a chip on his or her shoulder. Nor will it be a brash, no-nonsense type who never stops to listen. Think about it carefully, and you should be able to come up with a list of qualities which, you hope, you can highlight in your interview.

## Background to the company

Depending on the position you have applied for, it may be a good idea to do some background research on the organisation you have applied to for employment. Obviously, this is not always going to be appropriate or possible, but if it is a large multi-national to which you have applied it should be relatively easy to find out information on its activities. If it is a public company you can usually obtain a copy of the annual report from the company secretary at the head office. With smaller companies there is nothing to stop you from asking the company to forward you some literature about the company and its business. If this proves impossible the other alternative is to revisit your local reference library and ask the staff if you could look at any market-research information that relates to the kind of business your potential employer is in. For example, if the organisation you have applied for is a small family-run company manufacturing frozen foods or heating equipment you can find out about that area of business. Most reference libraries will carry this information but you will need to ask where it is in the library.

## Planning your journey

Not a problem if your interview is in your local town and you know precisely where your interview is being held. However, if it is further afield you need to plan your journey. How do you intend to get there? Do you know how long it will take? Check these unknowns out. If you are in a motoring organisation ask them for an ideal road route. If you have Teletext or Ceefax view the relevant text to see if there are any road works. Is your car in working order? The last thing you want is some last-minute problem which delays you. Have you enough petrol? Unless you have allowed for refuelling this might cause you an unscheduled delay. Have you put your maps in the car? Is it winter? If so, might it be frosty and will this delay you? Put newspapers on the windscreen. In short, try to eliminate anything which could cause problems.

If the train is a better alternative, check the train times and ask if there are likely to be any delays. If you decide on train as the best way, book your seat to ensure you at least can travel in some comfort.

On any journey of some distance try to build in a margin of error to allow for slight mishaps. Additionally, aim to get to the vicinity of your interview about half an hour before your designated time.

## What to wear

Give some thought to which clothes you want to wear well before your actual interview. You may need to ensure these are washed, ironed or dry-cleaned. Have these clothes together with any shoes ready the evening before your interview.

As to what kind of clothes are suitable to wear, obviously this will depend on the position for which you have applied. Remember that clothes and especially shoes give clues to what kind of person you are. This is the case whether you have applied for a cleaning job or a managing director's position. For example, if you were interviewing for a cleaner because you were concerned about the general standards of tidiness and cleanliness in your offices, which person would you employ, a person who turned up, buttons hanging off, scruffy jeans and scuffed shoes or a person although modestly dressed appeared to be neat, with clean, pressed clothes and polished shoes?

## The day of the interview

As we have already mentioned, if your journey is a long one aim to arrive half an hour before your interview in the vicinity it is to be held. You might need to pinpoint the building or find a place to park. Next aim to arrive ten minutes early in the reception area of your interviewer. Do *not* be late. It is downright rude and may be taken as an indication of your unreliability.

If you have followed our advice and arrived early put your time in the reception area to good effect. Are there any company publications or displays which give valuable information about the company? If so, flick through them. There may be a selection of trade magazines relevant to the market in which the company operates. Again, flick through them. There may be information about the company or, importantly, a competitor. Perhaps there is new legislation coming in which will have a significant impact on the industry? Extract what you can and use it to your advantage so as to appear knowledgeable in the interview. Is there an opportunity to engage the receptionist in conversation? If you are male we do not mean 'What's a beautiful girl like you doing in a place like this?' Rather, questions like, 'Are the phones always this busy?' You might get a reply like 'Well, it's the new product we've just launched'. In other words, use the opportunity to glean any useful information.

## Making a good first impression

When the time comes to meet your interviewer it is essential that you create a good impression. The circumstances in which you might meet your interviewer will vary and you need to be prepared for any one of the following situations.

Your interviewer might walk in to the reception to greet you. If this is the case, rise to meet him or her, introduce yourself and shake his or her hand. Alternatively, the receptionist may direct you to the room where the interview is to be held or you may be escorted to the room by another individual. In this situation walk confidently into the room and introduce yourself, stating your name and extending your hand for a handshake.

## The handshake

The handshake is very important. There is nothing worse than the 'clammy fish' handshake: wet, cold and limp. All this handshake does is convey the impression that you are a weak-willed and 'wet' individual. A variation on the 'clammy fish' is the 'Uriah-Heep' whereby only half the hand is gripped around the finger area. Again, not a handshake which inspires confidence.

If you have a problem with excessively sweaty palms make sure that you take the precaution of drying your hand immediately before the interview. There is currently a product on the market called 'Hands Dry' available from chemists. This will ensure your hands are dry for the handshake since it can be applied up to six hours before the interview. If you suffer from cold hands use common sense: attempt to warm them before your interview.

In short, your handshake should be firm and strong, but don't overdo it. You don't want your potential employer to think you're Robocop! A handshake that is too strong can suggest over-enthusiasm and a domineering attitude. Present your hand by extending your arm, ensure your grip is firm and full and look the person you are meeting fully in the eyes while smiling pleasantly.

## Sitting down and body language

The way you conduct yourself in terms of movement, posture and mannerisms in an interview situation will send signals to the interviewer. It is essential you send the right signals.

When you sit down in the chair offered to you do not be afraid of adjusting it slightly. Indeed, there is a school of thought which says you should do this as a means of demonstrating confidence. Let's be clear we are not proposing you drag the chair half way across the room. An adjustment of a few inches is more than adequate.

If you are carrying any baggage think carefully what you want to do with it. Under no circumstances 'dump it' on the interviewer's desk since this may well be regarded as an infringement of territory and very rude. Similarly, a handbag or briefcase placed between you and your interviewer may come to represent a real physical barrier.

Be sure to sit up straight, not stiffly but in a manner which conveys interest and alertness. By all means hold an item in your hands if this makes you feel less nervous and gives you something to do with your hands. However, at all costs avoid playing with whatever it is you are holding, as it will merely create a distraction and convey nervousness. Another sure sign of defensiveness is to sit with folded arms as though hugging yourself. Don't do it. It is perfectly all right to use your hands to make a point but don't overdo it. You don't want to look like a demented traffic warden conducting traffic on the Paris ring road.

Nerves can play havoc with your speaking style or highlight certain phrases. For example, whereas everyone says things like 'you know?', 'I mean', 'Okay?' or 'of course', there is a limit to how many times in a conversation they are acceptable. Likewise another mannerism encouraged by pressure is the nervous laugh after each statement.

There is a range of habits and mannerisms which are inappropriate in the interview situation. Are you a foot tapper? A nail biter? Do you constantly scratch your head, twirl and untwirl a strand of hair? If you are unaware of any mannerisms ask your spouse or some friends. If you have a camcorder record yourself in conversation. Either way you'll probably come up with a long list! Try to eliminate the more irritating and distracting ones.

One habit which is especially hard to handle is cigarette smoking. This is particularly so since an interview is precisely the sort of situation which is likely to have you reaching for a cigarette. Frankly, the best advice has to be do not smoke despite the need you might feel. It is increasingly the case that employers have a no-smoking policy and this is usually rigorously enforced. This situation has partially come about as the result of legislation as well as the growing recognition of the damage caused by 'passive smoking' to non-smokers. You have to be aware, therefore, that to many employers a smoker represents 'hassle' and it might count against you. You may well be offered a cigarette as a means of establishing whether you are a smoker. There is no point trying to disguise the fact that you are a smoker if you are unable to get through the day without smoking. If you do get the job this would only create problems. On the other hand, if you do really want the job you must consider giving up and whether in reality you can.

## Eye contact

The classic sign of a shifty person with something to hide is an unwillingness to maintain eye contact. It is basic common sense that you do not keep averting your eyes, a fact recognised by the many phrases in the English language underlining that truth. For example, 'look me in the eye and say that' or 'eye to eye'.

We are not suggesting you maintain a robotic stare but rather you should not lower your eyes or let them wander around the room. Lowering your eyes can mean shyness or deceit. Eyes roaming around the room can mean disinterest. When you make a statement look your interviewer in the eye. Similarly, when that person is addressing you, you should be looking at them. Some people have genuine difficulty maintaining eye contact. If you are such a person, instead try looking at an imaginary point in the centre of the person's forehead (almost as if you were a marksman lining up the rifle sights on an intended victim). In this way you appear to the person to be looking them in the eye without actually causing yourself any discomfort.

## Read

*Successful Interview Skills* (Kogan Page) 1992
*Winning at Your Interview* (Kogan Page) 1990

# 8
# The Interview

Before the real questioning begins the interviewer might engage you in polite conversation. For example, 'Did you find us okay?' or 'The weather's bad today, isn't it?' Whereas these may be innocent questions aimed at 'breaking the ice', your response to them will give your interviewer an indication of the type of person you are. If you are only able to mumble simple 'yesses' and 'noes' your interviewer may be forgiven for thinking you are a limited conversationalist. This may have a bearing on your suitability for the type of position you have applied.

Try to respond positively with replies like, 'The journey was quite good really, I was surprised at how few contra flows there were' or 'The train was only 20 minutes late, but I'd allowed for that in my timing' or 'Yes, you were fairly easy to find, I'd checked on your address in the A to Z yesterday'. Do not go to the other extreme of giving a rambling reply which describes everything in full detail. Nor do you want to encourage your interviewer to discuss matters which are irrelevant to your application. There might be a limited time available for you to get across your selling points. The more time spent discussing pleasantries the less you have available to you to achieve that.

As we mentioned previously the whole purpose of an interview is to determine whether you are suitable for the job. The interviewer can ask a range of different types of question to uncover relevant information about you. These fall into three broad areas:

- Experience and ability
- Personality traits
- Reasons and motivation for move.

To extract this information the interviewer can frame questions in a certain manner to create a situation which might cause you to answer in a way which might be unusual, ie catch you off your guard. We need to examine these methods so that you may be prepared for them. The different methods or styles of questioning may be detailed as follows:

1. Open and closed questions
2. Pressure questions

3. Moral dilemma questions
4. Tests.

You need to be prepared for any of three styles of questions and for this reason it is worth running through each style. Finally, we will examine methods of testing sometimes used to complement interviews.

## Open and closed questions

Closed questions are specific and can be answered by a straight 'yes' or 'no' or very short answers. Hence the term 'closed': the question does not demand an 'open' detailed reply. For example, 'So you were born in Preston?', 'Are you married?', 'Are you a smoker?', 'I see you passed an exam in Biology?' The purpose of such questions may be to check statements you have made in your CV. You can use the opportunity to expand beyond 'yes' and 'no' if you want to, for example, 'Yes I did very well in biology, I've always found it an interesting subject', or 'Yes, I was born in Preston, that's where my father was based with the army and that's how I gained my first interest in . . .' Closed questions can also be used to test your commitment, for example 'Can you work Saturdays?', 'Can you work overtime?', 'Can you work in a seven-day, three-shift system?' or 'You've got no problem sitting professional examinations then?' or 'Are you happy about relocating?'

Open questions are not quite as simple. They require more than a 'yes' or 'no' and consequently a lot more thought. It is quite acceptable to take a few seconds to think before replying to an open question. You may even ask a question yourself to clarify what answer is required. Examples of open questions are 'How do you envisage you would fit into the company?', 'What is your attitude to total quality management?', 'What were the reasons behind your leaving Jones Brothers and Co.?', 'How did you get on with your supervisor?', 'How do you feel about working with the general public?'

Although open questions require more thought they do give you an opportunity to present a favourable account. The way you choose to answer a question is revealing. The interviewer will therefore be evaluating your responses. It is important in terms of the overall image you present and you will benefit from prior preparation.

## Pressure questions

The job you have applied for might involve pressure or stress and the interviewer might consider it appropriate to test out your reaction to answering questions presented in a stressful way. Another possibility is that questions which create pressure might cause you to reveal information you wished to keep quiet about. There are a variety of techniques and we will consider each in turn.

Aggressive questions may make you feel you are being interrogated. The tone employed is usually bullying and confrontational. An example might be 'So you lost your last job because you basically couldn't get on with anybody', 'Sounds like you were out of your depth', 'What makes you think you could do this job?', 'So what you're saying is any job will do so long as you can leave Jones Brothers?', 'Looks like you're a job-hopper to me'.

Another tactic is to subject you to a steady burst of short, sharp questions. The interviewer will want to see how you will respond to this style of questioning and whether you will become flustered and be caught off balance. It is unlikely you will be subjected to this kind of questioning unless the position you have applied for is sales or customer-service related.

One other tactic under this heading is the 'technique of silence'. This is familiar to salespeople and is a variation of 'who blinks first loses'. In this situation an interviewer asks a question and waits for your reply. When you finish your reply, silence. The interviewer says nothing. You feel uncomfortable and decide to add a little more. Again silence. You are unnerved to add something else. In such a situation your mind can give ill-thought-out answers. An example might be:

> *Interviewer:* You've had three jobs in five years and you want to move on again. Why?
> *You:* To gain a broader experience of the industry. (*Silence.*) And there is no encouragement or incentive for career development at Jones Brothers. (*Long silence.*) My manager won't agree to any further training. (*Long silence.*) Basically he's very old fashioned and hasn't listened to any of my requests. It gets me down, he's so short sighted.
> *Interviewer:* So you don't get on with your manager?

This might be an area you had not wanted to discuss or reveal.

## Moral-dilemma questions

Moral questions can be very tricky and can lead you into a moral minefield which is precisely what they are meant to do. One classic is the famous, 'Which do you think is worse, someone who pilfers stationery from the office or someone who steals some cash from an old widow?' If you start answering with statements like 'Well, it depends how much was stolen' or 'Depends how well off the widow was compared to the company', you will be in trouble. The interviewer might follow up with 'So you condone theft in certain circumstances, do you? What circumstances are they exactly?'

Not only can moral questions show you to be a person of dubious morals they can also test how easily led you are. An example of both would be a question from the interviewer (leaning forward and conspiratorially): 'I don't like working with coloureds, do you?' or 'Women are okay to work with but they make lousy managers'. Questions which might be designed purely to lead you on would be, 'Every salesman I've ever met has been full of hype, don't you think so?' or 'I've never yet met an accountant with a personality.' With these kinds of question you must take great care not to fall into any kind of trap. Do not be afraid to disagree, politely but firmly. Such a response might well have been the one that was in reality expected. For example, 'Well, frankly the colour of a person's skin has never mattered to me, it's the personality that counts', the answer to that might be 'Well, I'm glad to hear that. Not only are we an equal opportunity employer but value the custom we get from the ethnic community in the area, it's very important'.

# Tests

There is a variety of test exercises which companies may use to determine your suitability for the position you have applied for. These may be summarised as:

- Psychometric tests
- Skill tests
- Group interactive tests.

## Psychometric tests

There is some controversy concerning the worth of these tests which purport to show personality types. Originally developed in the 1930s they are believed by one school of thought to be fundamentally flawed. American companies in particular seem to place great faith in them.

The tests work through a series of seemingly conflicting and random questions presented in a multiple choice format. From your answers a personality profile will be arrived at. You will be asked to choose descriptions which you think describe you. For example you might have to choose from: '1. I take great pleasure from classical music; 2. I always have to win in any game I take part in; 3. I dislike colleagues who bring their personal problems to work with them; 4. I always plan in great detail before starting a new project; 5. I am always the life and soul of the party.' By the constant repetition of similar questions in different configurations, a profile builds up.

It is not really possible to prepare for a test of this nature and your best advice is to answer in a manner you feel comfortable with as long as this is not likely to paint a picture of you which conflicts with the position applied for. For example, if the job you want will involve tough competitive leadership do not opt for those questions which highlight 'soft, caring, sympathetic' aspects, for example 'I love reciting poetry' might present the wrong image. Try to choose answers that highlight those aspects of your personality which relate to the job applied for.

## Skill tests

Usually these will be general tests designed to reveal the extent of your ability in a given area. For example, the paper might be designed to reveal your numeracy skills, your English language skills or your reasoning skills. Another example might check out your claims concerning speed typing or computer knowledge. The tests would normally be subject to a specific time deadline.

If you have discovered that you are likely to be tested in such a manner there are some common-sense steps you can take to improve your performance. If there is a numeracy test ensure you know your multiplication tables and revise calculation of fractions etc. If you have claimed a certain typing speed, practise before the test.

## Group interactive tests

You may be asked to join in with other interviewees and be given a variety of tasks. How you and your group perform will be assessed by the interviewer(s). Most common is the setting of a specific group task which must be completed in a certain time. The interviewers will determine how you interact with other people. Are you very domineering, perhaps a bully who will not listen to others? Are you someone who gives up trying to get a point of view across? How practical are you? Do you stick to the brief? Do you persuade or just follow? Are you a loner?

You might be asked to do a presentation to your group either on a set topic or one of your choosing. Again, a number of skills will be evaluated. Are you good on your feet? Are you confident? Does your presentation follow a logical pattern? Do you make use of presentational aids such as overhead projectors, noticeboards etc?

Again, the correct response to these scenarios is to apply common sense. In a group role-play situation, carefully try to assess what skills the job you have applied for will demand. Will they really want a bombastic railroader as their employee or the wilting non-player who has the right ideas but is completely sidelined?

For any presentation follow the very simple outline of a start, a middle and an end. State what your presentation will be about, say it, and then recap with your conclusions. Make use of either the boards or the projector if available. Speak clearly and from prepared notes. As with the interview itself, make sure you do not lapse into distracting habits.

## Read

*How to Master Selection Tests* (Kogan Page) 1991
*Test Your Own Aptitude* 2nd edition (Kogan Page) 1990

# 9
# Interview Questions: A Practical Example

This chapter attempts to give you some idea of the scope of questions that you may come up against in an interview. Obviously, this list is not exhaustive, it is merely intended to set you thinking. We have used a mixture of question styles and techniques referred to in the last chapter. Furthermore, we have divided the mock interview into different segments to provide you with clearly identifiable stages which cover the areas previously discussed. The stages are:

- The opening
- The chronological review
- The personality probe.

We have also identified the type of question which is being asked at any one time and included that in brackets at the end of each question.

## The opening

*Interviewer:* Hello, come in ...
*You (offering hand):* Hello, Richard Smith, pleased to meet you.
*Interviewer:* John Brown, pleased you could make it. Take a seat. Good trip down? (*Closed question.*)
*You:* Fine, there were no road works on the motorway and I made very good time.

## Chronological review

*Interviewer:* Excellent, well perhaps we can get down to business. I've read through your CV but I think it would be useful if we could go through it. Could you start with your first job? (*Rather than running through a fictitious CV imagine giving an account of your work experience. The questions asked contain examples of the different categories of questions we have covered in the last chapter.*) So you have an RSA II qualification? (*Closed question.*)

*You:* Yes.

*Interviewer:* What use have you been able to put it to? (*Open question.*)

*You:* It's been very useful in terms of my work with computers. I'm very fast at inputting. Also the course included learning basic computer skills.

*Interviewer:* So you covered computers? (*Closed question.*)

*You:* Yes.

*Interviewer:* You left college in 1986? (*Closed question.*)

*You:* Yes.

*Interviewer:* When you were at Riley's, how did you find supervising two teams? (*Open question.*)

*You:* I enjoyed the challenge and I certainly learnt a lot about time management and people management.

*Interviewer:* Would you say you were a good supervisor? (*Open question.*)

*You:* Yes, I think I was. The team's performance certainly improved. I was also able to tackle a couple of the team members' personal problems which were impacting on their work performance. I think being able to identify and resolve those sorts of problems is an important part of management. (*Towards the end the interviewer interrupts and decides to put you under a little bit of stress to determine what kind of person you are.*)

## The personality probe

*Interviewer:* So you left Jones Brothers because you didn't get on with anyone there?

*You:* No, I got on very well with my colleagues. I was keen to pursue vocational training qualifications but the company didn't have a training policy. I wanted to better myself.

*Interviewer:* Aren't you a bit old for this job? (*Pressure and open question.*)

*You:* No. I believe it's experience and ability that count and my career to date demonstrates that.

*Interviewer:* Your academic qualifications are pretty appalling, aren't they? (*Pressure and closed question.*)

*You:* Well, perhaps I should have applied myself more at school but the fact is I have an excellent grasp of this industry when it comes to practical matters ... and I'm a quick and willing learner. (*NB: Although the question was closed it demanded a rebuttal beyond a straight 'no'.*)

*Interviewer:* So you've had four jobs in six years, do you like moving around? (*Pressure and open question.*)

*You:* I believe in bettering myself and moved to make the most of my abilities. What's more, all the jobs have contributed to my experience and are relevant to this position.

*Interviewer:* Let me ask you this. Which do you think is worse, a lad who steals a fiver from an old widow or a lad 'taking' five-pounds worth of stationery from a big company? (*Moral question.*)

*You:* I was brought up to believe that all theft is wrong and I still believe that. Otherwise where do you draw the line?

*Interviewer:* What do you dislike most about your job?

*You:* The lack of career prospects and training.

*Interviewer:* Sounds to me like you're saying everyone's to blame but you?

*You:* Well, I . .

*Interviewer (interrupting):* You said you think your manager's useless, didn't you?

*You:* Actually . . .

*Interviewer:* You reckon the employer's no good because there's no training, that's what you said, didn't you?

*You:* What I . . .

*Interviewer:* So essentially you leave an employer when the going gets tough. What was it, four jobs in six years? (*Pressure and closed question.*)

*You:* Would you like me to answer those points now or are there any other questions you'd like to put to me first?

*Interviewer:* No, fire away.

*You:* First, what I said was that my manager and my company do not share my views on the importance of training. I want to develop my skills and I'm keen to learn new ones. There is just not the opportunity with my present employers. The only reason I have moved on from employer to employer is because of career development. There's nothing I would like more than to work for a company committed to the development of its employees.

# Recap

The questions we have provided above are obviously merely examples and your interview will probably be completely differ-ent. What is unlikely to be different are the kinds of questions and manner in which they are asked. The answers we have provided have one common characteristic: they are all 'confident' and this is the way you should approach any question. The interview is an opportunity for you to sell and market yourself and you must make the most of it.

Also consider your answers. Do not feel the need to reply the moment your questioner finishes speaking. This is particularly true of a question designed to create some kind of pressure. Before replying consider what it is that is being implied.

Consider constructing a dry-run interview before a specific interview takes place. We are not saying the whole interview should be rehearsed but you should certainly prepare yourself for the weak points. Construct a list of awkward questions on those weak points and then work on a number of suitable replies until you have got a reply that sounds right.

It is always a good idea to have a couple of questions to ask them at the end of the interview. These might relate to points not covered, such as when does the job start, what are the career prospects within the company or matters relating to the benefits package. Do not be afraid to ask how you got on and when you can expect to hear from them.

## If you fail!

Regard each interview as a test run for the one which will eventually get you a job. It is likely that your interview skills are rusty and you are quite simply on a learning curve. Try to analyse what it was that went wrong and ask the question, 'Why didn't I get the job?' Ring them up and find out, ask for their advice about where you went wrong. Most employers will tell you. You may find out there was nothing wrong, that it was a matter of your living too far away, it may be that you came very close and they will consider you for the next position that comes up. The key point is to learn by making contact and asking questions. If you do that instead of being 'crushed' by rejection you will eventually succeed.

### Read
*Great Answers to Tough Interview Questions* 3rd edition (Kogan Page) 1992

# 10
# Starting Your Own Business

## Is it a feasible option?

Ceasing to work for an employer provides you with the opportunity to consider starting your own business. The idea might appear daunting or perhaps you have often dreamt of such a development. You need to take a cool and objective look before plunging into any kind of venture. It may be you have a skill or interest which would readily provide a good base for a commercial venture.

The purpose of this chapter is not to provide you with the mechanics of setting up a new business but rather to examine the sort of options which may be presented to you. After all, this is possibly a worrying time for you and you should not embark on any venture out of desperation. Likewise, if you have received a lump-sum redundancy payment there will be many individuals offering all sorts of get-rich-quick schemes. This chapter is not intended to be negative. We merely ask that you remove the rose-coloured spectacles, consider the information covered and ask the appropriate questions.

## Categories of business

There are, in very broad terms, three categories of business activity which can be outlined as follows:

- Services or products supplied to large corporate organisations that require specialised skills. For example, software design, tax advice, market research.
- Services and products aimed at supplying manufacturers or wholesalers. In other words, selling business to business. For example, packaging materials supplied to a food manufacturer or car valeting to a garage.
- Selling services and products direct to the public via a shop, retail premises or advertisements.

When you did your SWOT analysis you should have identified your strengths in terms of current employment skills and your outside interests. Do these have an application in the context of self-employment? Where within these categories do they fit?

If your business idea fits in the first category, are you sure your skills are sufficient to be attractive to potential clients? Such businesses do not normally require commercial premises and you may consider working from home. This will limit your financial risk but can impair your earning ability if you are unable to work without constant interruptions from your children or neighbours, etc. You must discuss any proposal to work from home with an accountant since there can be both tax advantages and dis-advantages depending on your circumstances.

If your venture fits into the second category, you will face slightly different issues. Again, it is not always necessary to have commercial premises. However, it has to be said that many of these ventures demand increasing amounts of space and this may need to be accounted for. This category is probably the easiest to enter and for that reason is the most competitive. In any kind of competition there are winners and losers and the failure rate is highest in this category. You are also likely to face delays in payment and bad debts which can cause you serious cash-flow problems.

The third category relies on selling services and products to the public and consequently usually requires commercial premises. The location of the shop or pub, etc, can be critical to the success or failure of the venture. It is also likely to require an element of risk. On the other hand you should ask yourself if the business could be run on a mail-order basis or from home. For example, a mobile hairdresser or toys sold by mail order.

# Initial research

Before you can determine whether a business proposition is viable you need to ask yourself some questions and then set out to answer them:

- Who will be the clients?
- What is the competition?
- What does the competition charge?
- Is the competition laying people off?
- Is there a new competitor about to open up that will capture business?

If you do not know the answers to these questions you will need to conduct further research. Use your reference library to check out the trade you wish to enter. Detailed market research is held at main reference libraries published by Keynote, Mintel and the Economist Intelligence Unit (EIU). Read local business publications and local newspaper back-copies to find out about closures or new companies. Walk down the high street to see what the competition is like. Read through Yellow Pages to establish where your nearest competitor is.

# Predicting financial viability

You need to have some idea of the volume of business you can generate, ie how much you can sell or supply to how many customers/clients and over what timescale. Furthermore, you must set a price and from that work out what your gross income from sales will be.

## Determining profitability

Having determined what you think your sales income will be you need to work out what your profit will be. This is:

Sales – Costs = Profits

There are two types of costs, 'direct costs' and 'indirect costs', known as 'general overheads'.

## Direct costs

Direct costs are those which arise as a direct result of the supply of a product or service, eg the petrol used in delivering a package to a customer or the paint bought to finish 200 Russian dolls.

## General overheads

General overheads are those which apply once you set up a business and occur whether or not any service or product is supplied, eg the cost of the delivery van or the doll-factory rent. Typically they will include salaries, property rental, utility services, insurance, etc.

Do not be misled by equating profitability with 'gross margin'. Gross margin is:

Sales value – direct cost = gross margin

In other words, gross margin does not take account of the general overheads which have to be taken into account when looking at the viability of a business. It's common sense really but can often be overlooked. Financial control of a business is vital and therefore it is important that general overheads are not only identified as a total sum but are also calculated on a per-unit basis if relevant.

## The critical importance of cash flow

Many people seem to have a problem understanding just how

critical cash flow is to the survival of a business. Perhaps we can demonstrate its importance with analogy.

Imagine you are a farmer in country where water is scarce. To keep your crop alive you require 200,000 litres of water a year. To be successful your only criterion is the need to get access to water. In fact your calculations show you have easy access to 300,000 litres a year. Can you keep your crop alive and your farming business going based on this criterion? The answer is 'perhaps'. If the water is available from a steadily flowing river fed by many tributaries and not subject to seasonal change then the answer is 'yes'. However, if the farmholding is situated next to a dry river bed in the desert which receives a once-only monsoon-type flood the answer is 'no'. The fact is the farmer needs a constant supply of water. Any serious interruption to flow could destroy the crops and the business. So it is with the cash flow of a business.

Cash flow is all about the timing of income and expenditure. It is no good being profitable on paper if there are bills to be paid and money is not yet in to pay them. Your business will be insolvent. The amount of money you need to keep going is known as working capital. The amount of working capital needed is likely to increase as the business expands.

Many a company has actually been brought down by success! As the demand for their goods has increased they have expanded production or taken on new staff. This has meant an outlay in, say, buying more materials. If there is too big a gap between paying for those materials and receiving payment for the products you have sold, the company is insolvent. This gap is the working capital requirement and must be forecast so you can make adequate provision.

### Will the business provide an income?

The whole purpose of considering starting a business is to provide you with an income you can live on. Does your business do that? It is quite possible your business will only be profitable after a year or two years. As long as you have allowed for that in your projections this is not necessarily a problem. It is an area you would need to discuss with your accountant.

This sort of research and planning is fundamental and allows you to approach your business idea objectively.

## Identifying possible business ventures

Perhaps your original idea was not feasible but you are still interested in setting something up. Or perhaps you do not feel you have any particular skills which could form the basis of a business venture but feel self-employment is the only feasible option open to you. If either scenario is relevant to you this section should help you source business opportunities. We have divided this into three categories:

1. Existing businesses
2. Franchises
3. Multi-level marketing.

We will examine where you can find opportunities in each of these categories, and provide relevant information about the type of businesses which are to be found within these categories and the pitfalls you can face.

## Existing businesses

You will find existing businesses for sale in a variety of publications. National and local newspapers may advertise businesses for sale. *Exchange & Mart* lists all kinds of businesses for sale as do various trade magazines. Small high-street businesses often attempt to sell their premises as going concerns through estate agents.

Buying an existing business can have its advantages. You cut out the set-up stage and, you hope, inherit contacts and clients. Often the sale price of the business includes something called 'goodwill' which is an unquantifiable value calculated on the fact the business exists as an entity. You need to take a long hard look at the business which is offered for sale. Ask yourself the following questions:

- Why is the business for sale?
- Is the business based on very personal contacts which will vanish with the current owners?
- How realistic is the goodwill? Is it a try-on?
- Is something about to happen which will impact on trading? (For example, is a new supermarket opening? Is the factory whose workforce are your customers closing down? Is a rent review due? Are double yellow lines about to be positioned outside the shop?)
- Are the assets really owned by the company and are they worth anything? When were they valued? Have they been depreciated?
- Are you going to be responsible for debts if you buy it as a going concern?
- Is there stock involved? Is it valued realistically or is it unsaleable?

It is unlikely you can answer these questions on your own and you will need to take professional advice from solicitors and accountants.

There are two types of business opportunities which tend to head the lists of ex-employees considering starting up on their own: running a pub and owning a village post office. For that reason we think it worth while elaborating on what is involved in each of these. We cannot give you any specific financial advice but we can attempt to give you a flavour of what running one of these businesses is actually like. It is better that you are fully aware of what is involved before you sink your redundancy pay into a venture which, although it might be financially viable, is at odds with your view of what life would be like.

Let us examine the public-house venture first. You might have a rosy view of what running a pub is like. Perhaps you have an image of yourself as the genial host quaffing ale with the regulars as the world goes slowly by. However, your day may go something like this. First, your day can start as early as 7 am with the delivery of stock. (You might have deliveries every day.) Before this can be done, 'bottling-up' must take place. This is the process whereby all 'empties' are removed and replenished with checks against your inventory. Are you fit enough to carry possibly 50 crates, each equivalent to a large sack of potatoes, possibly up from the cellar? When delivery is taking place you will need to keep an eagle eye on what is going on to ensure no pilfering takes place.

How good a cook are you? Pubs make most of their profit from food. Your morning tasks could include making sure you have got sufficient stocks in. Who is to cook and serve the food? If you employ people, what happens if they let you down? At what point in the day will you be doing their wages and the bookkeeping? These are all tasks which you might well have to deal with before opening at, say, 11.30 am. When you close after that (if you do) you will have more checks to perform and more bottling-up.

When you open up again for the evening trade the process repeats itself until, say, 11.15 pm and cleaning up starts. Of course, there is the bottling-up but perhaps you can get up early, say 6.00 am, and do that before delivery. Of course, all this assumes an uneventful day. There could have been a visit from any number of public servants: HM Customs and Excise (the VAT man), Health and Safety, Trading Standards, Environmental Health or even the Drugs Squad. You might have a problem with a drunk, a fight over a girl, obscene graffiti in the loos or an overflowing toilet.

If you can cope with this sort of lifestyle then perhaps owning and running a public house is for you. All we are saying is that a pub is a business and as such a full-time ongoing commitment is required and you must be aware of that before you commit yourself to such a lifestyle.

A few words about the 'village post office syndrome'. Again, there is a tendency to overlook just what is demanded. If you are considering buying one which is both a general stores and a newsagents you should be aware of the demands which the business will make on you. The bookkeeping demands will be considerable and the times you will be required to open daunting. There is the risk of holding cash because although theft in rural areas has been small, recent years have seen a growth in crime in seemingly isolated communities. If you sell newspapers, are you prepared to open up every morning to mark up and sell them (deliveries are usually between 5.00 am and 6.30 am)?

Then there is stock control. How good at it are you? Buy too much of one food item and you might be left with it on your shelf past its sell-by date. Buy too little of something too often and people will cease coming to the shop for that kind of item. Do you like your holidays? If you will want to take some, who will be looking after the shop? Again, as with running a pub, it is not just a question of whether something is financially viable – it is a question of whether you can adapt and accept the kind of lifestyle involved.

## Franchises

A franchise is a licence sold by a business to another entity allowing that entity to participate in that business activity. Usually, the company which is offering the licence (the franchisor) has successfully operated the business and is now offering the idea together with support to anyone prepared to pay the asking price. A number of franchises are usually offered and these will be for specific regions or towns as the company selling the franchise will be keen to ensure that whoever buys the franchise has exclusive rights to operate in a given area without competition from that company or another franchise. Essentially a franchise offers you a package of 'inside information', the necessary equipment/expertise, the brand name of the company, ongoing marketing support and advice.

There are a large number of high-street franchises which are household names. Indeed, you may be surprised at how many businesses you thought were branches of large companies are in fact owned and run by local operators. Some leading ones are Dyno-rod, Wimpy, ProntaPrint, Hometune, BSM Driving School, Spud-U-Like, Gino's Pizzas and California Car Wash.

The franchise concept is great for those individuals who feel that they have the necessary skills to run their own business but feel they lack any special knowledge which they can make into a business. A good franchise offers you entry into a trade about which you might know very little. The provision of technical information, training and back-up have made it possible for many individuals to buy franchises in areas of trade in which they knew nothing and then run successful businesses.

In order that you can appreciate how a franchise might operate we will examine one of the most popular franchises, high-street printing and copying services. First, if you are interested in buying a franchise to open a print shop in your town, the company selling the franchise will check to see if there is a 'vacancy'. If the town is covered by another operation in their organisation they will inform you and offer some 'free' areas. Assuming your town is free and you proceed, they should conduct some research to establish whether the business is viable in that area and what business will be produced. They will then help you locate suitable premises. Once you are located they will fit out the premises in the 'group' colours. Normally the franchise fee will include capital equipment and the initial payments on equipment covered by leasing agreements.

All the equipment you need to operate will be provided. Usually the fee includes initial marketing and advertising costs. It may also include an allowance for salaries. While the refurbishment is happening you will have attended various training courses dealing with aspects of the business. When you return from your training you should find premises ready and you can open your doors and start trading. All this is what is known as a 'turnkey' operation, ie you are purchasing a complete ready-to-operate package.

In addition to the initial cost of the franchise you will also pay the franchisor an annual fee based on turnover (not profit), usually around 6 per cent. This is meant to contribute to the central corporate branding costs. Both the initial and recurring costs of a quality franchise can appear to be high. Usually you would only be expected to fund a deposit. The reputable franchises have financial packages agreed through the banks which will fund the difference.

### *Where to find out more about franchises*
Franchise opportunities are advertised in a variety of publications. Local and national newspapers will carry advertisements for them under 'business opportunities'. There are whole magazines dedicated to franchise opportunities. These are available from your newsagents, your library or even your local Employment

Centre. You will find the variety and scope of opportunities massive with entry costs ranging between £5,000 and £500,000.

## Are franchises good value?

The first point to make is there are good franchises and outright 'rip-offs'. There are some basic questions you need to ask yourself when examining a franchise opportunity:

- Is the business tried and tested?
- What is the competition like in the area you will operate?
- How well established is the brand name? (ie, had you heard of the company before you started looking for a potential franchise?)
- What corporate advertising is there?
- Are the premises to be owned by you or bought by the franchisor and leased back to you?
- How good does the back-up seem?
- How much are you expected to pay to them each year?
- Are you committed to use the franchisor as a supplier of certain materials even if you can find cheaper suppliers?
- How long do you have to stay with the franchisor? Can you break away after so many years and go independent?

You can see from these sorts of questions it is absolutely vital to bring in specialists to advise. Some high-street banks have managers who specialise in franchises.

Even with the most respectable franchise there is a suspicion that you are paying an awful lot more than the component parts add up to. The truth is you don't get something for nothing. You will be paying a premium for what can be called 'goodwill' and that could be as much as half again of the actual costs of setting the business up. What you are paying for is knowledge, expertise and back-up. What price can you put on these because, without them, you would have lacked the means to have entered your chosen trade?

## Multi-level marketing

If you read the 'business opportunities' pages of newspapers it is quite likely you will see various references to 'earning opportunities'. Usually the details are vague but mention full- and part-time work earning significant sums of weekly income. Alternatively, you may be approached by a friend or colleague who is anxious to share a great money-making opportunity with you. The chances are this is 'multi-level marketing', sometimes known as 'network marketing'.

### The background to multi-level marketing

The origins of the present-day multi-level marketing system can be traced back to schemes which were known as 'pyramid selling'. Pyramid selling hit the UK in the 1960s and caused a lot of people to buy stocks of various products which they were unable to sell. It was such a huge 'rip-off' that legislation was brought in to make certain practices illegal and control any pyramid schemes so as to protect participants in the scheme. Multi-level marketing has grown from the old form of pyramid selling and as long as it conforms to government legislation is entirely legitimate. It is most unlikely that any of the current schemes on the market do not conform to British law.

### Multi-level marketing and the law

To protect individuals from the bad practices of pyramid selling, the government brought in legislation to regulate multi-level marketing operators. The relevant legislation is part XI of the Fair Trading Act 1973, the Pyramid Selling Scheme Regulations 1989 and the Pyramid Selling Schemes (Amendment) Regulations 1990. We will go through your rights at a later point in this chapter.

### What is multi-level marketing?

If you were to join a multi-level marketing scheme you would be offered the opportunity of buying a range of products or services from the individual who recruited you or from the company running the scheme. In turn you will be able to sell these products to the public at a price which gives you a profit. In addition you are expected to recruit other individuals who will purchase stock and go out to sell to the public. They too will recruit and the pattern repeats itself. A network or pyramid builds up comprising salespersons. Any sale made by someone you recruited and, for that matter, anyone whose recruitment can indirectly be traced back to you, will benefit you in the form of a commission. Likewise any sale you make will not only benefit you but also the people above you who receive a commission.

### How exactly do you earn money?

This is a difficult area and it is worth recapping. There are a number of ways in which you can earn money in a multi-level marketing operation:

● You can earn money on the goods you sell. So you buy a product for £10 and sell it for £15.
● You may receive a bonus for selling a certain amount of stock within a certain time period.

- If you recruit someone else as part of your 'network' you might get commission on any sales they make.
- You might get more bonuses or bigger discounts by getting 'promotion', which usually means recruiting so many or selling so much stock.
- You might get income by providing training or other services to participants.

### Will multi-level marketing suit you?
The first fact you must acknowledge about multi-level marketing is that it is about selling. It is about persuading individuals to buy your product and join your network.

Many different kinds of people have been successful in multi-level marketing schemes both in terms of selling and recruiting. There are three factors which will determine whether you will be successful:

- The nature of the scheme.
- Are you a salesperson?
- Is there a market for the product?

### The nature of the scheme
Every scheme will be different although the mechanics will be similar. Before you agree to commit any money to a multi-level marketing scheme you need to check out precisely how you earn money. What are the buying and selling prices of the product? The 'margin' which you earn on each product should always be identifiable. In this way you can calculate how many you need to sell to generate the income you require. Remember it is likely that this margin will vary upwards or downwards depending on the quantity sold. When you have calculated how many you need to sell to generate the required income you must satisfy yourself that this is possible at the recommended retail price.

Any scheme which places undue influence on recruitment at the expense of direct selling is suspect. If the sole intention is to persuade new recruits to buy stock there is a danger the product is weak and there is actual difficulty selling it retail.

### Are you a salesperson?
The whole idea of multi-level marketing is that you use established friends and contacts to sell the scheme's products to. You are therefore selling to a receptive and friendly market. To a degree it is true to say that you do not need superb selling skills. The question you must ask yourself, however, is whether you would be comfortable approaching friends and neighbours with the product in question. Often it is not the idea of approaching such contacts but the actual product you are attempting to sell. You might feel

silly trying to sell perfume but happy selling diet/health products or vice versa.

### Is there a market for the product?

When you attend a multi-level scheme meeting you will be shown the incredible earning opportunities open to you. Graphs will be produced showing massive untapped market potential. Try to keep your feet on the ground. What is being said may be true but try to apply some common sense. Remember we live in an economy known as a market economy. This means that when the demand for a certain product or service is present then the market will ensure demand is met. Quite simply, suppliers enter the market and, in an attempt to achieve greater market share, compete with one another. Apply this general concept to what you have been told about the market for your product. If there really is a massive market just waiting to be supplied, what is the competition doing? What are their products like? How much are competitors' products? In a recession, how necessary/vital is the product to people?

If the scheme you are joining has been established for some time, have you joined too late? (Your area might be saturated.) This is a difficult question to get answered and you might be told it is not relevant. It is relevant because unless you have family in another part of the country where the scheme has not yet reached, you might find your local friends and neighbours already know about it.

### Points to look out for

Before you join a scheme make sure you have written information about it and a written contract which contains a statutory warning. The statutory warning should state that it is advisable to take independent legal advice before signing. The terms and conditions must include the right to pull out of the scheme without penalty if you return the unsold goods within 14 days. The scheme promoter does have the right to deduct any monies due and, after 14 days, deduct monies to take account of deterioration if this is as a result of your negligence.

Any scheme which requires you to invest a sum of £75 or more as the fee for joining is illegal. This sum also includes any money you are asked to pay for stock. The scheme promoter is able to sell you goods in excess of this sum when you have been in the scheme for more than seven days.

As we have already stated, beware of any scheme which uses the promise of fantastic earnings based purely on recruiting others and if the intention is to persuade you to put a lump-sum investment into the scheme.

Treat with suspicion any scheme which attempts to make you pay for your training. You must be told in advance what the costs are. Secondly, a good scheme should provide free training, otherwise there has to be a suspicion that the activity is just a means of making more money.

Have a look to see what cars the organisers of the scheme are driving. If they are really earning lots of money they should have the lifestyle to go with it. All too often these so-called high earners are driving around in clapped-out bangers. Do not be fooled by their showing you huge commission cheques. Often they have to make payments from this cheque to others in their downline. Also, if you attend a multi-level meeting watch out for how much stock there is around. If supposedly the stock is selling well or should be out on demonstration, why is it sitting around?

Finally, if you have any remaining doubts it is worth contacting your local trading standards office (under your council in your phone book). Ask them if they have heard of the scheme and for their views.

# Ways of running your own business

There is one other aspect of running a business you need to consider before you decide to proceed. This aspect concerns the legal format and has far-reaching financial implications. The categories are:

- Sole trader
- Partnership
- Co-operative
- Limited company.

We will examine each of these in turn and comment on their advantages and disadvantages. We will also mention briefly the tax and National Insurance implications of each.

### Sole trader

The title is self-explanatory: it simply means you are the sole person trading. You are totally responsible for all decisions, all debts and all profits. It also means that all your assets both personal and business related are at risk if your business fails. In other words your liability is not 'limited' in any way, it is total. That is why some sole traders ensure that personal assets are not in their own names.

You are regarded as self-employed by the Inland Revenue and as such will be on a different tax schedule. If your business fails you will find that your former self-employed status excludes you

STARTING YOUR OWN BUSINESS    **101**

from receiving many State benefits. The advantages of being self-employed lie in the fact you are able to use personal and business assets legitimately and claim costs.

You do not have to use your own name if you are a sole trader as this might not always be appropriate in marketing terms. But if another name is used you must show that you are the owner. For example, you might be known as 'A Jones trading as Speedy Parcels'.

## Partnership

Again, a term which is self-explanatory and similar to the status of 'sole trader'. A partnership is two or more persons joined together in a commercial venture. As with the status of sole trader you are not limited in your liability if your business fails. It is possible to come to an agreement with the other partners concerning the division of profits and benefits but not liabilities. You must ensure any partnership is bound by a comprehensive agreement, preferably drawn up by a solicitor. The agreement must cover points such as who has authority to sign cheques, how many signatures are required, how often cheques can be issued and for what amount. The agreement must also define what unilateral decisions can be made by a partner (if any) by way of financial commitments. If these issues are not tackled and a partner makes a disastrous financial commitment on behalf of the partnership, all partners are liable.

## Co-operative

Co-operatives are run and owned by the people who work in the business. Co-operatives are usually set up as companies limited by guarantee (see below) or as an industrial and provident society. You must all share responsibility, make decisions equally and usually all receive equal pay. Think about these points carefully. Equal pay is good if everyone contributes their best, but what happens if someone does not pull their weight? Also, decision-making can sometimes be difficult.

## Limited company

A limited company is a legal entity which is owned by its share-holders and run by its directors. Limited companies can be bought 'off the shelf' from companies who advertise in the quality press. Quite simply you can purchase for around £150 a virgin entity and issue shares of £100 and appoint yourself a director employed by the company.

This means you have legally separated yourself as an individual from the business. Your liability is therefore limited to the money you have invested in the form of shares. So if the company collapses the creditors cannot come after the owners (shareholders). However, it is often the case that creditors will require personal guarantees which means you would become liable for that particular company debt in the event of company failure. For example, if your company leased some equipment, the lease company would probably only have agreed to underwrite the deal with a guarantee from you as an individual.

If you set up a company and appoint yourself as a director in receipt of salary you are deemed to be an employee. You are not self-employed since you are working for a different legal entity from yourself. It is advantageous to have been an employee rather than self-employed from the benefits' perspective if your business fails.

## Help in setting up your business

We have already discussed the Training and Enterprise Councils (LECs in Scotland) in Chapter 5. However, in addition to their vocational training role they are also charged with two other functions which directly relate to the establishment of businesses in their areas. These are:

- Provision of business advice and training;
- Administration of Business Start-up Scheme; and
- Enterprise initiatives.

We will examine each of these in turn.

### Provision of business advice and training

As we explained, each TEC or LEC covers a specific geographical region and gears its provision of services to meet the training and skill demands of the local economy in question. Consequently the provision will vary from place to place as will the methods. But you should find that, at the very least, your TEC or LEC can give you business advice and counselling concerning the setting-up and running of your proposed venture. They will also make available a free planning kit which gives you the fundamentals you will need if you are to raise finance, etc. You will also be offered a variety of training opportunities relevant to your needs.

### Business Start-up scheme

This replaced the Enterprise Allowance Scheme and is administered by the TEC or LEC and they decide whether you are eligible, the amount you should receive and for how long. The intention is to use the money effectively to provide those new ventures which have a real chance with the optimum start by giving you an income until the project is self-funding.

## Enterprise initiatives

The calibre of TECs and LECs varies widely and will be reflected in the range of ideas and services they offer above the basic two we have mentioned. If you are fortunate enough to live in an area where the TEC or LEC is genuinely entrepreneurial and innovative you might find all sorts of useful initiatives. For example, 'Business Angels' is a concept started by the Devon and Cornwall TEC which puts wealthy sponsors in touch with new ventures needing start-up capital. The West London TEC has pioneered the idea of making a professional expert in personnel matters available to growth companies for 20 days over a six month period.

## Contacts

Business in the Community
8 Stratton Street
London
W1X 5FD
Tel: 071-629 1600
(Will provide you with details of enterprise agencies in your area.)

Freephone Enterprise
Tel: 0800 222999
(Free connection to your local Small Firms Centre who will provide information, counselling and advice about business matters.)

Graduate Enterprise
Room W825
Moorfoot
Sheffield
S1 4PQ
(Will give you details of regional centres to help graduates with a business idea.)

Instant Muscle
84 North End Road
London W14 9EF
Tel: 071-603 2604
(A charity established to help unemployed young people set up in business.)

Livewire
Freepost
Newcastle upon Tyne
NE1 1BR
Tel: 091-261 5584
(Gives money for 16–25 year olds for business start-ups.)

Prince's Youth Business Trust
1st Floor
5 The Pavement
Clapham
London SW4 0HY
Tel: 071-498 3939
(Grants to young people wanting to run their own business.)

## Read

*Working for Yourself: The Daily Telegraph Guide to Self-Employment* 15th edition (Kogan Page) 1994

# 11
# Working or Retiring Abroad

This chapter attempts to offer some general advice on your rights abroad and the opportunities for employment which exist there. Increasing numbers of UK citizens either retire abroad or gain employment overseas. Usually there are sound economic reasons for this process. Obviously, the situation varies depending where overseas you are considering, and this chapter cannot hope to cover every circumstance. We have therefore attempted to give an overview of rights and opportunities with close attention to those regions and areas most popular with British citizens. The considerable advances in the European Community in respect of employment and retirement rights are also covered.

This chapter is divided into the following main sections:

1. Employment in the European Community
2. Retirement in the European Community
3. Working outside the European Community
4. Retirement outside the European Community.

## Employment in the European Community

### The European Community – your rights as an EC citizen
As a citizen of the EC you have the right to seek and obtain employment within the EC. You will not need a work permit. However, since most EC states require their nationals to carry identity cards you are required to carry a full British passport. You will normally also be required to obtain a resident's permit. This is to ensure you are registered as a 'local' and so you have access to the rights enjoyed by other nationals of that state. These rights concern pay, working conditions, social security, access to housing, vocational training and trade-union membership. If your family is to join you, then they would be entitled to similar rights.

### Getting a job in the EC
You cannot be refused a job in an EC member state on the basis of not being a national of that state if you are an EC citizen. This rule applies to both the private and public sectors. There are some

restrictions relating to public service jobs if the job in question relates to matters of national security, etc. Of course you can be refused a job on the basis of inadequate skills or poor language understanding.

To find vacancies there are a number of channels open to you. The European Enrolment Services System (known as EURES) is one method you could consider. This was set up in 1970 and makes available a computerised database of vacancies across the EC. It is accessed in Britain by calling in at an employment centre and asking a member of staff to access the system. The database is known in the UK as 'NATVACs'. It is capable of checking whether there are any matching vacancies for your skills using agreed EC job descriptions. If you locate a vacancy in which you are interested and receive an application form then, unless specified, you will be expected to complete it in the language of the host country.

## Unemployment Benefit

If you have been in receipt of UK Unemployment Benefit for at least four weeks and remain eligible to receive the benefit you may have this paid to you for up to three months while you look for work in other EC states. You must, however, register for work in the member state where you are looking for work within seven days of arrival. Furthermore, before you leave the UK you are expected to give your Employment Centre five working days' notice of your intentions. They will issue you with a form which you will need to present at the Job Centre in the EC member state you are looking for work in.

## Health and social security

You are entitled to receive medical treatment free but you must have completed the necessary documentation prior to travelling outside the UK. The documentation is not difficult to complete and is available from all post offices and is called form E111. Failure to have completed this will mean you are charged full rate for any medical treatment you receive. Forms T2 and T3 explain your rights in terms of medical treatment.

You may wish to consider taking out private medical insurance which you can obtain through insurance brokers. If you are currently covered by private medical insurance this is unlikely to provide cover for extended periods of stay. Also, you must check that the level of cover is high enough to cover private medical treatment in the country you are proposing to live in. You must specify that it is not travel cover you require and ask if the cover is set at UK scales of charges and whether this is sufficient.

## Compatibility of qualifications

The EC has made major headway in ensuring qualifications and practical experience gained in one member state are measured against a European standard and thereby given recognition throughout the EC. A series of EC directives have ensured that many UK professional and vocational qualifications are given comparability and are recognised.

The Department of Trade and Industry has drawn up a list of 'regulated' professions in a booklet called *Europe Open for Professionals*. A regulated profession is one whose practice is regulated in some way by law, administrative regulations and provisions in a member state. So in the UK regulated professions include accountants, teachers, lawyers, physiotherapists, psychologists, chemists, engineers, surveyors, ships brokers, etc. This means that your professional qualifications are recognised in the EC. If you belong to a profession which is not regulated in the UK but is in another EC member state you will still be entitled to practise that profession if you can demonstrate you have worked in that profession for a minimum of two out of the previous ten years following three years of postgraduate study.

With regard to vocational qualifications, the EC has produced a list of occupations where the vocational qualifications are accepted across the EC. The NVQs and SVQs (levels 3/4) form part of what is known as 'regulated education and training'. It is qualifications such as these which are covered by the EC directive. Occupations covered by the EC directive include motor mechanic, auto electrician, vehicle body repairer, auto paint-sprayer, painter and decorator, roofer, carpenter, joiner, waiter/waitress, chef, porter, bricklayer, glazier, hotel receptionist, stonemason, floor tiler, concrete worker and others.

If you want more information about this aspect of working abroad you can contact:

The Comparability Co-ordinator
Occupational Standards Branch/OS5
Room E454
The Training Agency
Moorfoot
Sheffield S1 4PQ
0742 704144

If you require general information about working abroad you should contact:

The Overseas Placing Unit
Employment Service

Rockingham House
123 West Street
Sheffield S1 4ER

Any questions about your professional or vocational qualifications can be answered by the DTI's European Division on 071-215 5610.

# Retiring in the European Community

As we have said, UK subjects are now deemed to be citizens of the EC. Increasing numbers of UK subjects have already decided that the warmer climes and lower living costs are worth moving for. Spain and Portugal have large British communities and you might be surprised at the network of support which exists for such groups. So substantial is their presence that local radio and newspapers in English have developed to service their needs. Spain in particular has undergone rapid modernisation and fears about the standard of healthcare facilities is no longer the concern it might once have been.

Of course many people are reluctant to sever their links completely with the UK. You may have friends or family still there. Consequently, many people opt to maintain a small flat as a base in the UK as well as an apartment abroad.

## Pension rights

Basically there are no problems in receiving your UK State pension if you are living in the EC. It is paid at exactly the same rate as if you were in the UK. It is normally paid by payable orders sent at four-weekly or quarterly intervals either direct to you or alternatively into a bank/building society account either in the UK or abroad.

## The effect of early retirement

If you have taken early retirement and are looking at the possibility of living abroad you need to consider the impact of your ceasing to make National Insurance contributions. Retiring early in the UK would allow you to continue to sign on (or go on a period of interruption, see Chapter 2). But you cannot get NI credits automatically if you are abroad for more than six months (182 days) in any tax year.

If it is your intention to go abroad for six months each year (or you have already done so), you need to make a claim for Unemployment Benefit so that your NI contribution credits are safeguarded for the period you are in the UK. You then have the option of paying voluntary class contributions for the period you are out of the UK. These Class 3 contributions will safeguard your rights to a statutory retirement pension and, if you are a man, your wife's widow's pension. Check out what these will be: you might find they do not add up to very much.

## Health and sickness

If you go to live in an EC country you will be entitled to the health services of the sickness insurance institution of that country. If you have been in receipt of Sickness Benefit from the UK this can be paid for the duration of the entitlement, to you, in the EC country of residence.

# Working outside the European Community

The first point to make is that this is such a wide category it is difficult to offer many meaningful generalisations. There are, however, a number of points which are of some relevance. Unlike the EC, UK subjects are unlikely to have any automatic right of abode or employment. This is as true of what can be called the 'White Commonwealth' as it is of anywhere else. We mention this because of the common misconception that somehow British people have an automatic right of entry to their old colonies.

A distinction must also be made between an arranged job abroad, that is to say, one which is offered to you by either a UK employer or foreign employer, and a job you intend to obtain by entering the foreign country. Bearing in mind what we have just said about your 'right' to employment, this is likely to be 'unofficial' employment.

## 'Unofficial' employment

Perhaps a more accurate title might be illegal employment. Many Brits enter countries on tourist terms and decide to stay on and gain work. This is particularly true of those English-speaking countries with whom the UK has traditionally enjoyed close ties, such as the USA, Canada, Australia and New Zealand. Unless the job you are performing requires some unique skill possessed by no native of that country, it is most unlikely you will receive a dispensation to work there. Once your tourist visa has expired then your status as an illegal immigrant will obviously cause problems in the context of tax and insurance schemes to which you and your employer should be contributing.

## Arranged employment

If you have been offered a job working abroad your circumstances abroad will depend on whether the job is temporary or whether it is more long term and involves emigration. If you are working for a UK employer but on an expatriate contract basis, your status may be different from an open-ended job offer by a foreign company. In either of these instances the terms and conditions of your employment should have been well defined in advance. If your position is permanent it is likely that you will be treated in the same manner as an indigenous taxpayer which will, of course, vary depending on the country you are employed in.

### Paying National Insurance contributions

The UK has agreements with many other countries apart from those of the EC (we have listed these at the end of the chapter). You should contact the DSS to enquire about the country that is relevant to you. For example, in the situation where you are employed by a UK company but working abroad you and your employer might still be liable for Class 1 National Insurance contributions for one year. This arrangement would exempt you from paying into the local insurance scheme.

### When National Insurance is not paid

National Insurance may not be payable if your employer does not have a UK base or if no agreement exists between the countries.

### Making voluntary National Insurance contributions

If you are not obliged to make NI contributions while working abroad, you ought to consider making them on a voluntary basis. Most people are entitled to make these contributions while living abroad but there are conditions, the most important of which is the requirement that you must have lived in the UK for at least three years. If you are eligible to make voluntary contributions you have a choice of either paying:

- *Class 2*. These count towards UK Sickness Benefit, Maternity Benefit, basic retirement pension and Widow's Benefit; or
- *Class 3*. These count for basic retirement pension and widow's pension.

# Retirement outside the European Community

There are two circumstances which need to be considered:

- early retirement
- UK State pensions and benefits.

## Early retirement

The country to which you want to retire will have its own unique entry and residence requirements. It is likely that these will include restrictions on individuals who are without the means of independent financial support. Your pension income will there-fore be assessed to determine whether it is deemed sufficient. Obviously, the amount will vary depending on the policies of that country and the cost of living. Another factor might be whether you have any relatives living in that country. These are issues of immigration policy and are only mentioned in passing. For further information you ought to contact the relevant embassy or consulate.

## Off-shore accounts

If you intend to retire abroad and live off a pension or investment income you need to investigate the possibility of establishing an off-shore account into which your income is paid before onward payment to you.

## UK State pension and other benefits

When you reach retirement age but are resident in another country, the amount to which you are entitled will depend on whether an agreement exists between the UK and the country of your residence. You will therefore need to contact the DSS to determine what arrangements there are. It is impossible for us to detail every possible situation but we have included a brief guide to the pension situation in the most popular retirement destinations outside the EC.

### Australia

If you are intending to retire to Australia your UK retirement pension may be paid there but only at the rate in force when you were last resident in the UK. If you first become entitled to the pension after having left the UK for Australia, it would be paid at the rate which applied in the UK at the time of your entitlement. All the above applies to the widows' pension.

Unless you are an approved migrant you will not qualify for free treatment under the Australian equivalent of the NHS, known as Medicare. In this situation you would need to take out compre-hensive medical insurance.

### Canada

Similar to Australia in that UK retirement and widows' pensions are payable to people living in Canada but only at rates which were current either when they left the UK or when they first became eligible if they were already living in Canada. *No subsequent increases in the pension are payable.*

You are not entitled to any medical cover or for that matter any other State benefit.

### Cyprus

Quite simply, if you live in Cyprus you are entitled to your UK benefit at exactly the same rate as if you were living in the UK. The same applies to the widows' pension.

As far as medical cover is concerned, there is no reciprocal cover and you must therefore ensure you have cover. If, however, you were to return to the UK and a medical condition occurred then you would remain entitled to NHS treatment.

### Malta

You can receive a UK retirement pension at the same rate as if you were in the UK.

Medical treatment is not covered except for British visitors.

### New Zealand

If you were entitled to a retirement pension when you emigrated to New Zealand, it will continue to be payable at the rate which you were receiving in the UK. If you first become entitled to the pension after leaving for New Zealand, you will be paid at the rate which applies in the UK when you became entitled.

The agreement with the UK is perhaps the closest of any of the ex-colonies and as such may entitle you to qualify for other New Zealand benefits including 'National Superannuation'. The agreement allows you to treat residence in the UK as residence in New Zealand.

Treatment is available to you under the New Zealand Health Service which is similar to the NHS. However, it is normal to pay a consultation fee for a GP or specialist but there is no prescription charge. Recent changes have included the introduction of a fixed daily charge for hospital treatment. These charges are paid by all New Zealanders but the NZ Department of Social Security may refund some.

## Read

*The Expatriate's Handbooks* (Kogan Page) 1993
*Good Retirement Guide 1994* (Kogan Page) 1994
*Living Abroad: The Daily Telegraph Guide* 7th edition (Kogan Page) 1994
*Working Abroad: The Daily Telegraph Guide* 17th edition (Kogan Page) 1994

# 12
# Investing for the Future

Obviously this chapter is not going to be of any relevance if you are not in the fortunate position of having received a large lump sum. It does, however, contain useful information about the types of scheme which are worth knowing about for the future.

If you do have a lump sum which you received as part of a redundancy payment, this chapter should certainly be relevant. However, you must appreciate it would be illegal for us to give you any specific financial advice. We are able to detail the types of investment schemes which are available and which you may wish to explore. As we have stressed previously, each individual's circumstances and priorities are going to differ and this will determine what is appropriate and what is not. For example, if you have received a lump-sum redundancy payment and are fortunate enough to walk into another job you can perhaps afford to be more long term in your investment than someone who might need to live off their capital.

## Tax issues

There are three circumstances when monies paid to you in a lump sum are regarded as being tax free:

- When the money paid relates to termination due to accidental death, injury or disability of the employee.
- In a situation where the employee has spent most of his or her employment abroad.
- When you receive a lump sum other than in the above two situations it will attract tax above £30,000, eg redundancy or breach of contract. The first £30,000 is tax free.

### Situations where tax is payable

In the last situation we mentioned that tax is payable on lump sums above £30,000. The following should be noted. Although the first £30,000 is regarded as tax free, do not forget that any statutory payment you receive will contribute towards the first £30,000. Similarly, any other benefit such as the gift of a company car to you will be valued by the tax office and included in the total. Therefore it is quite easy for the £30,000 allowance to be eroded and tax be applied on a figure of less than £30,000. You should also be aware that tax will almost certainly be applied at the higher 40 per cent rate.

## Avoiding tax

It follows that your pay-off must be constructed carefully if you are to avoid paying tax. Of course, this assumes that your ex-employer is willing to be flexible. That said, there is an incentive for your ex-employer to play ball since tax you save also saves your ex-employer employer's National Insurance contributions.

The main way to avoid paying tax is to ask for any sum over £30,000 (after allowing for all monies and benefits you are to receive) to be made over directly into an approved pension scheme. This may not be an option if you envisage needing as much capital as possible to live off. If this is the case timing is the key.

Assume you need as much capital as possible and the sum does come to more than £30,000. Ask for your P45 to be issued before the lump-sum payment from your employer. If this happens your employer is not obliged to deduct tax at 40 per cent for any sum over £30,000. Instead your employer can apply it at 25 per cent, which means you gain a temporary cash-flow advantage.

## Maximising benefits

We have already covered this point but it is worth mentioning again. You will not get Income Support if you have savings of £8,000. You will get reduced Income Support if you have savings of £3,000. However, if you were to structure your redundancy lump sum to be paid into a pension scheme, you might avoid these 'excluding' criteria.

# Investing your money

The key question you must decide is, 'how liquid do you want to keep your funds?' As we have already stated, do not tie up your capital until you are certain you know what your cash demands are going to be.

## Gross interest savings accounts

This scheme applies to bank and building society accounts and is aimed at those individuals who are not using their tax allowance because they do not have sufficient income. In the past interest was taxed at source and the net amount paid to the investor.

Since 1991 you can claim back the tax difference if you have not used your allowance. Although you are almost certain to have used up your allowance, what about your spouse or your children? Obviously, you have to have a good relationship if you are to consider this option.

If your spouse is not liable to tax at all, they register to have their interest paid gross on form R85 available from banks and building societies. The same applies to your children. If there are any earnings but the full personal allowance is not used up, the gross interest element is claimed back at the end of the tax year or when you are owed more than £50.

A deposit of around £50,000 at 7 per cent per annum would enable you to utilise fully a single-person's allowance (currently £3445). Obviously, the size of the sum can vary without breaching the allowance. It will vary depending on the rate of interest paid and the size of the personal allowance.

Do not be tempted to put the account in joint names as the Inland Revenue will treat half the interest income as yours and half as your spouse's. The interest will be taxed on yours but not your spouse's. The effect is to reduce the 'efficiency' of the scheme by 50 per cent.

In terms of liquidity and appreciation, this is a winner and one which you should consider. The scheme applies to any savings account and you will have to determine which of those is suitable. Check out the best savers' rates (gross) by visiting building societies or by buying the *Mail on Sunday*, which lists the best deals. Alternatively, consult Oracle on Channel 4 for still more detailed information. Do not forget building society 'postal accounts' which normally pay extra. Try not to lock yourself into 90- or 120-days notice accounts unless you are confident of dealing with this length of notice.

## Pension plans

Although we have alluded to tax advantages of paying lump sums into pension plans we consider it important to elaborate on this point. The common perception is that the benefits one can expect from a pension plan arrive a long time after the payment is in. This is not necessarily the case if you are near retirement age. For example, a 60-year-old can pay a lump sum into a pension plan, receive tax relief (at their appropriate rate) and be able to draw benefits out immediately. You are able to draw out 25 per cent of the pension fund as a personal tax-free fund. The pension fund can start making payments immediately for the rest of your life and you do not have to be retired. Obviously, the amount you will receive will depend on how much you put in and the age you started drawing. Also be aware that any pension income may exclude you from State benefits. (See Chapter 2 where this is discussed in detail.)

## Tax-exempt special savings accounts (TESSAs)

We have included a description of this type of account not because we think it likely to be appropriate but rather because it is often confused with the tax rebate system that operates with ordinary savings accounts as described above. Basically a TESSA is open to any individual over the age of 18 and resident in the UK. Consequently husbands and wives may each have their own TESSA. In return for certain restrictions and conditions, interest will be paid free of tax. The restrictions and conditions are that the schemes run for five years with no withdrawal of capital, and the maximum investment allowed over a five-year period is £9000. Furthermore, in the first year you may only invest a maximum of £3000 followed by annual investments not exceeding £1800 until the total of £9000 is attained. If any capital is removed from the TESSA then all tax-free rights are lost. You are allowed to withdraw any interest at any time but you must keep a sum equivalent to the tax you would have paid on the amount you withdrew in the account. You may withdraw this at the end of the TESSA. At the end of five years the account reverts to a normal account, attracting tax deductions as any other would.

A TESSA is unlikely to be your best option if you have a spouse or children with personal allowances. However, if you are single and expecting to work very soon, or your spouse works, then a TESSA may be an answer as long as you realise the benefits depend on your capital being tied up for five years. The same applies if you receive any form of income.

## Personal equity plans (PEPs)

These were introduced as a means of encouraging wider share ownership by allowing a tax-free way of investing in shares. When you normally invest in shares you are taxed on any income you receive by way of dividend payouts. If the shares rise in value and you sell them you will be taxed for capital gains (assuming you have used up your capital gains allowance). With PEPs all income and capital gains are tax free.

The maximum amount you can invest in a PEP is £6000 each tax year and, since everyone is treated as an individual, both a husband and wife can each have their own PEP every year. Investments can be by way of monthly payments or a single lump-sum payment.

Imagine a PEP as a basket in which you can put a variety of

different investments. These are shares, investment trusts and unit trusts. The shares are restricted to UK shares quoted on the stock exchange and certain shares quoted on EC member state stock exchanges. There is a restriction of £3000 per year on the amount of investment trusts and unit trusts which may be allowed in your PEP 'basket'. Of these, at least 50 per cent of the investments must be in UK or EC shares. However, you are allowed to invest in trusts that do not meet this requirement but only to a total of £1500 instead of the £3000.

As well as the normal £6000 annual allowance, you are allowed an additional £3000 for shares of a single company. This is highly relevant if you have already acquired shares in the company you once worked for and/or if you have accepted shares or share options as part of your redundancy package. By placing them in a single company PEP, you will avoid tax on any income.

PEPs are run by plan managers who are authorised to do so by the Inland Revenue. The shares owned by you are administered by them and for which charges are deducted. It is worth shopping around to find the lowest management charges. For example, they can vary from an initial charge of 5 per cent to 0.25 per cent.

## Friendly societies

Friendly societies have special tax privileges which have been granted by the government. These allow you to invest a lump sum in a tax-free savings plan which is unit-trust endowment linked. Every individual (including children) can have a plan. The sum you can invest is limited to £200 each year. The payments can be made monthly. The plan is usually for ten years and the proceeds are tax free.

## National Savings

There is a range of plans and schemes available from National Savings which are free from both income tax and capital gains tax. These include premium bond prizes, fixed interest and index-linked savings certificates, yearly savings plans and the first £70 of annual interest on a National Savings Bank ordinary account.

## Enterprise Investment Scheme (EIS)

This replaces the Business Expansion Scheme and is aimed at stimulating investment in industry in general and manufacturing in particular. Unlike BES it does not cover investment in private rented housing.

Investors will get 20 per cent income tax relief on qualifying investments up to £100,000 in any tax year. But in its first year

(1994) relief for BES and EIS together will be a maximum of £40,000. Gains on shares will be exempt from Capital Gains Tax. It will also be possible to have a shareholding and be a paid director of an EIS company.

If you want to know more about any of the investments you are recommended to take independent financial advice. Do not go to an agent who is tied to one particular finance company if you want an objective overview. For a list of independent financial advisers near you write to:

The IFAP Centre
Studio House
Flowers Hill
Brislington
Bristol
BS4 5JJ

## Read

*A Consumer's Guide to Lump Sum Investment* 5th edition (Kogan Page) 1993

# Index

*add* = address

'A' level GCE 45
A/S (Advanced Supplementary) levels
    45
abroad, living 70, 105–112
    employment 105–8, 109–10
    retirement 108–9, 110–12
academic qualifications 44–5, 46–7
ACAS (Advisory Conciliation and
    Arbitration Service) 16; *add* 20
Advanced Supplementary (A/S) levels
    45
advertising, job 65–7
advice, business 102
Advisory Conciliation and Arbitration
    Service (ACAS) 16; *add* 20
age barrier, alternatives to jobs 69–70
age of retirement, women's 24
agencies, employment 62–3
aggressive questions 80
appearance, for interviews 74
arranged employment 109–10
Australia, UK benefits in 111
avoiding tax on pay-offs 114

background research, for interviews
    73
benefits
    employer 41
    state 20, 21–32, 114
        abroad 106, 111–12
        proposed future changes 31–2
bills, cutting 34–5
body language 76–7
British Trust for Conservation
    Volunteers (BTCV), *add* 70
BTCV (British Trust for Conservation
    Volunteers), *add* 70
BTEC (Business and Technology
    Education Council) 45
business
    activity categories 88–9
    advice 102

'Business Angels' 103
Business in the Community, *add* 103
Business Start-up scheme 102–3
Business and Technology Education
    Council (BTEC) 45
Business Training 52
'bust', employers who go 12–13

CAB (Citizens' Advice Bureaux) 36
cafeteria benefits 41
Canada, UK benefits in 111–12
career development loans 50, 52
Careers & Occupational Information
    Centre (COIC), *add* 53
careers offices 62
cars, company 20
caseworkers 32
cash flow 90–91
Ceefax 67
Central Bureau, *add* 71
Certificate of Pre-Vocational
    Education (CPVE) 46
Child Care Allowance 30
chronological review stage, interviews
    84–5
cigarette smoking 76–7
Citizens' Advice Bureaux (CAB) 36
closed questions 79, 84, 85, 86
clothes, for interviews 74
COIC (Careers & Occupational
    Information Centre), *add* 53
Commission for Racial Equality
    (CRE), *add* 20
Community Charge 25
Community Service Volunteers
    (CSV), *add* 71
companies, limited 101–2
company background research 73
company cars 20
compulsory redundancy 12–13
conduct and reasons for dismissal
    17–18

constructive dismissal 16
consultants, recruitment 63–4
  executive search 64–5
contracts of employment 14, 15
co-operatives 101
corporate organisations, services or
    products for 88, 89
correspondence courses 45, 48
costs, and financial viability 90
Council Tax 25
CPVE (Certificate of Pre-Vocational
    Education) 46
CRE (Commission for Racial
    Equality), add 20
credit cards 35
creditors, priority 34
CSV (Community Service
    Volunteers), add 71
customised CVs 57, 62
CVs 55–62
  examples 58–61
Cyprus 70
  UK benefits in 112

daily organisation, for unemployed
    68–9
*Daily Telegraph* 66
dead, claiming for someone who is 28
degree qualifications 46–7
demographics, and recruitment trends
    40
Department of Employment 42, 50;
    add 49
Department of Health, add 49
Department of Social Security (DSS)
    21–2, 24, 33; add 32
Department of Trade and Industry
    (DTI) 107, 108
  European Division 108
dependants' benefit 26
Devon and Cornwall TEC 103
direct costs 90
directors, company 102
Disability Advisory Service 32
disablement benefits 30
discretionary awards, education 48–9
dismissal 14–18
  legal advice 35–6
  procedure 16–18
  redress 15–16
  *see also* redundancy
distance learning 45, 48
DSS (Department of Social Security)
    21–2, 24, 33; add 32

DTI (Department of Trade and
    Industry) 107, 108

E111 form 106
early retirement 12, 13–14
  abroad 108–9, 111
EC *see* European Community
education *see* training
Educational Counselling and Credit
    Transfer Service (ECCTIS 2000),
    add 53
EIS (Enterprise Investment Scheme)
    117–18
employment 55–71
  abroad 105–8, 109–10
  alternatives to 69–70
  CVs 55–62
  organising your day 68–9
  sources 62–7
Employment Action 52
employment agencies 62–3
Employment Benefit Offices 32
employment capabilities analysis
    37–9
Employment Centres 33, 62
Employment Department 42, 50; add
    49
Employment Protection
    (Consolidation) Act 1978 14
Employment Rehabilitation Service
    42
Employment Service, add 107–8
Employment Training 52
enterprise initiatives 103
Enterprise Investment Scheme (EIS)
    117–18
Equal Opportunities Commission
    (EOC), add 20
EURES (European Enrolment
    Services System) 106
*Europe Open for Professionals* 107
European Community 40, 41,
    105–9
  employment in 105–8
  employment outside 109–10
  retiring in 108–9
  retiring outside 110–12
European Enrolment Services System
    (EURES) 106
executive search consultants 64–5
existing businesses, buying 92–4
expenses, travel to interview 29
Extended Jobplan 31
eye contact 77

factory noticeboards 67
failed interviews 87
Fair Trading Act 97
Family Credit 29–30
financial resources, conserving 33–6
    household and personal finances
        33–5
    legal advice 35–6
    lump sums 36
    settlements 18–20, 114
    viability, predicting 90–91
financing training and education
    48–50
first certificates and diplomas 45
first impressions, at interviews 75–7
flexible benefits 41
food bills, cutting 35
franchises 94–6
free training 48
Freephone Enterprise, add 103
friendly societies 117

GCSE (General Certificate of
    Secondary Education) 44–5
general overheads 90
Graduate Enterprise, add 103
grants 48–9
gross interest savings accounts
    114–15
gross margin 90
gross misconduct 17–18, 19
group interactive tests 82–3

handshakes 75–6
'headhunters' 64–5
health services abroad 106, 109,
    111, 112
higher education 46–7
Higher Grades (Scotland) 45
HNC/Ds (Higher National
    Certificates and Diplomas) 45–6
home, working from 89
household finances, conserving 33–5
housing costs, and Income Support
    24, 25

IFAP (Independent Financial Advisers
    Promotions), add 118
impressions, making good 75–7
income, of own business 91
Income Support 22, 24–5, 31, 114
Independent Financial Advisers
    Promotions (IFAP), add 118
indirect costs 90

industrial tribunals 15, 28
insolvent employers
    and occupational pension schemes
        28
    and redundancy 12–13, 27
Instant Muscle, add 103
interactive tests 82–3
interests, pursuing 70
International Voluntary Service (IVS),
    add 71
interviews 72–87
    example 84–7
    making good first impressions 75–7
    preparing for 73–5
    purpose 72
    questions 78–81, 86–7
    tests 81–3
    travel expenses 29
Invalidity Benefit 25–6
investment schemes 113–18
    tax issues 113–14
    types 114–18
IVS (International Voluntary Service),
    add 71

job clubs 28–9, 42
job prospects assessment 37–43
    analysis of capabilities 37–9
    choosing the right job 42
    recruitment trends 39–42
job review workshops 42
job seminars 29
Jobcentres 32, 33, 42, 62
'Jobfinder' service 67
Jobfinder's Grant 31
jobs
    alternatives to 69–70
    choosing the right 42
    sources 62–7
    state assistance to obtain 28–30
Jobseeker's Agreement 31
Jobseeker's Allowance 31
journeys to interviews 73–4
    expenses 29

knowledge workers 40

learning methods 47–8
LECs (Local Enterprise Companies)
    51–2, 54, 102–3
legal advice 35–6
Legal Aid 35, 36
legal format of businesses 100–102
liability, limited 101–2
life insurance 35, 36

limited companies 101–2
Livewire, *add* 104
loans 49–50
local
  education authorities 53
  newspapers 66
  radio 67
Local Enterprise Companies (LECs)
    51–2, 54, 102–3
lump-sum payments 12, 22, 36
  investing 113–18

Malta, UK benefits in 112
mandatory awards, education 48–9
mannerisms 76
manual workers 40
manufacturers, selling to 88, 89
manufacturing sector decline 39–40
market research 89–90
McKinsey, recruitment trends 40
'means testing' 24, 31
medical
  insurance abroad 106
  treatment abroad 106, 109, 111,
    112
misconduct 17
moral-dilemma questions 80–81, 86
morale 68–9
mortgage interest payments 24, 25
multi-level marketing 96–100
  background and scope 97–8
  suitability 98–9

NACRO *see* National Association for
    Care and Resettlement of
    Offenders
names, business 101
National Association for Care and
    Resettlement of Offenders
    (NACRO), *add* 43
National Certificates and Diplomas,
    BTEC 45
National Council for Vocational
    Qualifications (NCVQ), *add* 53
National Insurance (NI) contributions
    21–2, 26
  while abroad 108, 110
National Savings 117
National Vocational Qualifications
    (NVQs) 46
NATVACs 106
NCVQ (National Council for
    Vocational Qualifications), *add*
    53

negotiating leaving deals 18–20, 114
'network marketing' *see* multi-level
    marketing
New Zealand, UK benefits in 112
newspapers 65–6
NI *see* National Insurance
    contributions
noticeboards 67
nursing bursaries 49
NVQs (National Vocational
    Qualifications) 46, 107

occupational pension schemes and
    insolvent employers 28
Occupational Standards Branch,
    Training Agency, *add* 107
off-shore accounts 111
Open College 47
Open Learning, *add* 53
'open learning' 47–8
open questions 79, 85
Open University 47–8; *add* 53
opening stage, interviews 84
'opportunities' (SWOT analysis) 38–9
organisation, while unemployed 68–9
overheads, general 90
Overseas Placing Unit, Employment
    Service, *add* 107–8
own business, setting up *see* self-
    employment

paramedical grants 49
partnerships 101
'pay-offs' 18–20, 114
pensions
  occupational and personal 13–14,
    19, 22–3, 115–16
  state 30
    while abroad 108, 111–13
PEPs (personal equity plans) 116–17
performance reasons for dismissal 17
period of interruption of employment
    (PIE) 23–4
personal allowance, Income Support
    25
personal equity plans (PEPs) 116–17
personal finances, conserving 33–5
personality probe stage, interviews
    85–6
PIE (period of interruption of
    employment) 23–4
post office ventures 94
postgraduate education 47, 49
premiums, Income Support 25

presentations, at interviews 82–3
pressure questions 79–80, 85–6, 87
Prince's Youth Business Trust, *add* 104
priority creditors 34
private medical insurance abroad 106
professions, 'regulated' 107
profitability, determining 90
psychometric tests 81–2
public, selling direct to 88, 89
public house ventures 93–4
'pyramid selling' 97
Pyramid Selling Scheme Regulations 97

qualifications 44–7
  compatibility in EC 107–8
questions, interview 78–81, 84–7

radio, local 67
recruitment
  consultants 63–4
  trends 39–42
redundancy 11–13, 15, 25
  compulsory 12–13
  statutory 13, 26–8
  voluntary 11–12
references 20, 57
regional job newspapers 66
'regulated education and training' 107
'regulated' professions 107
research, self-employment 89–90
resignations 18–19
restart courses 29
retirement
  abroad 108–9, 110–12
  age for women 24
  early 12, 13–14

savings
  accounts 114–15
  and Income Support 24, 114
Scottish Certificate of Education Higher Grades 45
Scottish Vocational Education Council 45
search consultants 64–5
self-employment 12, 69, 88–104
  business categories 88–9
  help 102–3
  identifying possible ventures 91–100
  initial research 89–90
  predicting financial viability 90–91

running own business 100–101
self-esteem 69
selling multi-level marketing 98–9
seminars, job 29
share-option schemes 20
sickness abroad 106, 109, 111, 112
Sickness Benefit 25–6, 109
signing on 33
Single Market 40, 41
sitting down, at interviews 76–7
skill tests 82
skilled workforce needs 40–41
'slobbing out' 68–9
smoking 76–7
Social Fund payments 30
sole traders 100–101
speculative job enquiries 67
sponsorships 49
state assistance, obtaining jobs 28–30
state benefits 20, 21–32
  abroad 108, 111–12
statutory redundancy 13, 26–8
'strengths' (SWOT analysis) 37–8
stressful questioning 79–80, 85–6
student loans 50
Sunday newspapers 66
SWOT (strengths, weaknesses, opportunities and threats) analysis 37–9

TAPS *see* Training Access Points
Tax-exempt special savings accounts (TESSAs) 116
tax issues, investment 113–14, 115
Technical and Vocational Educational Initiative (TVEI) 46
'technique of silence' 80
TECs (Training and Enterprise Councils) 51–2, 54, 102–3
telephone bills, cutting 35
Teletext 67
temporary work 63
termination of employment 14–18; *see also* redundancy
TESSAs (Tax-exempt special savings accounts) 116
tests, selection 81–3
'threats' (SWOT analysis) 38–9
trade press, job advertising 66
Trades Union Congress (TUC), *add* 20
trained workforce needs 40–41
training 41–2, 44–54, 102
  financing 48–50

learning methods 47–8
TECs 51–2, 54, 102–3
types of qualification 44–7
Training Access Points (TAPS) 47;
add 53
Training Agency, add 107
Training Credits 51–2
Training and Enterprise Councils
(TECs) 51–2, 54, 102–3
transfers of businesses 13
travelling to interviews 29, 73–4
tribunals, industrial 15, 28
truth, in CVs 57
TUC (Trades Union Congress), add
20
'turnkey' operations 95
TVEI (Technical and Vocational
Educational Initiative) 46

UCAS (University and College
Admissions System), add 54
unemployment
daily organisation 68–9
voluntary 18–19, 25
see also dismissal; redundancy
Unemployment Benefit 21–4, 30,
31
in European Community 106

unfair dismissal 15
University and College Admissions
System (UCAS), add 54
'unofficial' employment 109

ventures, identifying possible 91–100
existing businesses 92–4
franchises 94–6
multi-level marketing 96–100
verbal warnings 16
village post office ventures 94
vocational qualifications 45–7
in EC 107
voluntary
employment 69–70
redundancy 11–12
unemployment 18–19, 25

warnings, disciplinary 16–17
'weaknesses' (SWOT analysis) 38
West London TEC 103
wholesalers, selling to 88, 89
women, retirement age changes 24
word of mouth, job opportunities 67
written warnings 17
wrongful dismissal 15–16

Youth Training (YT) 51–2